DREAMING SOURCE
OF CREATIVITY

THE
DREAMING SOURCE
OF CREATIVITY

30 CREATIVE AND MAGICAL WAYS
TO WORK ON YOURSELF

AMY MINDELL

Lao Tse Press
Portland, Oregon

For information contact:
Lao Tse Press
2049 NW Hoyt St., Suite 5
Portland, OR 97209
(503) 222-3395
(503) 227-7003 (fax)
www.laotse.com

Distributed to the trade by:
Independent Publishers Group
814 N. Franklin St.
Chicago, IL 60624
(800) 888-4741
(312) 337-5985 (fax)
www.ipgbook.com

Printed in the United States of America

Cover design: William Stanton
Book design: Heiko Spoddeck
Author photo: Aleksandr Peikrishvili

Mindell, Amy
    The Dreaming Source of Creativity:
    30 Creative and Magical Ways to Work on Yourself
    Bibliography
    Includes index.
ISBN: 1-887078-73-8 (pbk.)
Library of Congress Control Number: 2005929213

Contents

Playful King

Acknowledgments vii
Prologue: Life as the Canvas...ix
Introduction: Plant a Seed and It Will Grow 1

PART I: SEEDS OF CREATIVITY 11
    Chapter 1: The Intentional Field 13
    Chapter 2: The Essence of It All 29
    Interlude: Dreaming While I'm Awake................................ 41

PART II: FLIRTS AND THE LIFE OF MATERIALS 51
    Chapter 3: Flirts and the Land of Murk and Magic 53
    Alarm!   "I'll do it later" or "You could do it better"........ 69
    Chapter 4: Socks 75
    Interlude: So Close but So Far Away 89
    Chapter 5: It's Alive! 93
    Alarm!   "I Don't Know the Next Step" 105
    Chapter 6: Flirting with the Environment 109
    Chapter 7: Behind the Mask 117
    Interlude: Stop or Go 133
    Chapter 8: The Flying Umbrella Story 137

PART III: PARALLEL WORLDS AND CREATIVITY 147
   Chapter 9: Stepping into the Life of Someone Else 149
   Chapter 10: Musical Parallel Worlds 163
   Interlude: Lazy Dog 173
   Chapter 11: Dreambody Puppets 177

PART IV: CRITICS AND BIG ENERGY 197
   Chapter 12: It's All a Bunch of Junk! 199
   Chapter 13: Moody Misery 207
   Chapter 14: Making a Mess... 215
   Chapter 15: The Simple Path 221

Conclusion.. 229

Bibliography 231

Index... 239

ACKNOWLEDGMENTS

Rock Band

My puppets and I extend our deepest thanks to everyone who has inspired and supported me on my creative path.

I can hardly thank and appreciate Arny, my partner and husband, enough for his boundless support of my creativity. He has always encouraged me to believe in my dreams and even to go way beyond them. He has welcomed my music, crafts, and puppet beings into our home with open arms, has joyously joined me whenever possible in creating all kinds of fun creatures and songs, and has always encouraged me to explore and share my creative inspiration and ideas with others. The way in which Arny follows his own fount of creativity with utter devotion has inspired and touched me in more ways than I can ever express. His development of Process Work, his most recent explorations of the connections between physics and psychology, and his concept of the Intentional Field have formed the very foundation upon which this work is built.

Many thanks to Margaret Ryan, whose wonderful editing and joyful spirit have always helped and inspired me.

Great thanks go to everyone in our seminars who experimented with various aspects of this book as well as to those courageous and fun-spirited folks who participated in my wild and sometimes out-of-control classes! Special thanks go to those people who generously allowed me to use photos of their creations in this book.

I would also love to thank each and every person individually who has contributed to this book directly or indirectly. However, I found that as soon as I started to write each individual's name, the list began to multiply into dozens of names! I realized suddenly that it would be impossible to name each and every one of you. So let me say that I deeply thank my friends and students in Portland, Oregon, and around the world who have taught me a great deal and who have been willing to jump in and experiment with me. I also want to thank my colleagues with whom I have taught classes over the years and who have shared in this creative adventure. I have cherished the enthusiasm, co-creativity, and encouragement that each one of you has given me. I am also greateful to all of the artists, performers, and teachers who have inspired me and who have shown me that the world can be renewed and dreamed again and again.

Finally, I thank the Intentional Field that constantly guides and moves me; the fabric, glue guns, and musical notes that help to bring the unnamable to life; and the playful child in each of us who knows how to grasp and unfold the magical sparks of life.

PROLOGUE
Life as the Canvas

A few years ago my partner Arny and I were in the midst of preparing a seminar we called Stone Songs. The seminar would focus on accessing the vibrations and music in the body as a source of wellness and healing. As preparation for the seminar, I began to read the work of Sufi mystic Hazrat Inayat Khan, *The Mysticism of Sound and Music*. Khan's words spoke to me about the connections between music, the universe, and our lives. I remember being struck powerfully by a particular sentence (though, at the time, I wasn't quite sure why it affected me so strongly) in which he speaks about giving up music:

> I GAVE up my music because I had received from it all I had to receive. To serve God one must sacrifice the dearest thing, and I sacrificed my music, the dearest thing to me.[1] [emphasis in original]

Going Back in Time

Before going further, allow me to drift back in time for a moment. During my childhood and adolescence, I was involved in many creative activities, ranging from playing piano and guitar to singing and making crafts, from dance training to painting, from cooking to writing poetry. Later on, as a process-oriented therapist and teacher, my creativity bloomed in the form of my private work with clients and the classes that I taught (and continue to teach) alone and together with Arny. The wide ranging applications of Process Work afforded me a new kind of freedom from which I could bring many of my creative interests to bear. Any one session might include an ensemble of methods—from movement to artwork, deep bodywork to relationship work, social-change work to dialogue with toys and puppets.

The foundation of Process Work springs from the ancient Taoist beliefs in the wisdom and continual unfolding of nature. In

Essence, Process Work focuses on what nature is presenting in any given situation. As practitioners we seek to follow and adjust to that flow in our work with individuals, couples, and groups. During the last ten years I have written books and articles about Process Work themes. I found writing to be a particularly challenging task as I struggled to discover this new form of creativity in terms of using words to express process-oriented ideas.

Losing My Voice

Around my fortieth birthday I started to have trouble using my voice. My throat was often sore and I was frequently hoarse. This was quite difficult for me because we often lectured, and I spoke most of the day with my clients. It was also becoming difficult for me to sing—a limitation I took very hard because I had always adored singing. I had learned to play guitar and piano as a child just so that I could sing the most passionate songs of my favorite songwriters. Singing always felt like home for me, a place to transcend everyday life, to connect with my deepest feelings, and to reach for something much greater than myself. When I read Inyat Khan's words about sacrificing the dearest thing to him, his music, they moved me deeply.

Then something strange occurred. In the void that my voice no longer filled, in that vast emptiness that felt so barren and lonely, something new arose. I began to *hear* music—this time, my *own* music. It began to flow out of me like a plant that had finally gotten water and could at long last stretch out its roots into the soil around it. Until that time I had never been able to compose songs, and this lack had always frustrated me. Now I heard music in my mind and realized that actually it was not *my* music but came from some other source, something much larger than myself. I tried to get out of the way, listen to its melodies, and then transcribe and express them in voice and instrument.

I don't know why this happened when I turned forty. Perhaps the many years of *wanting* to write music needed to first wear itself out. Perhaps it was aging, a midlife transition. And maybe I was becoming more and more tired of my ordinary identity and could open up to the unknown. I don't really know.

Puppets

Then another wave went through me. A few years ago I was seized by a desire to make puppets. Ask any of my friends and they will tell you that I have since been totally possessed by the desire to create funky puppets of all kinds. I have managed to fill our house with so many puppets of different sizes and shapes that we can hardly get in the door anymore!

During these last few years I created a musical puppet theater and started to incorporate my puppets and music into my teaching and our seminars. I used the puppets and the process of creating them to demonstrate various Process Work methods and theories. I hoped to share the idea that psychology can be fun and that dreaming and imagination are essential and central aspects of a creative life.

The Intentional Field

Around the same time that I was exploring music composition and puppetry, Arny returned to his earlier studies of theoretical physics and began to draw numerous connections between physics and psychology. From his studies of the quantum wave function he came up with the term *Intentional Field*. He described this field as a generating, creative force that is always present within and around us and which we can experience by becoming aware of the slightest tendencies within and around us in any given moment. In our seminars he and I began to experiment with how the Intentional Field is experienced. I then began a series of classes on the how the Intentional Field can be understood as the seed of creativity. Those classes and our studies form the foundation for this book.

Life as Our Canvas

Things have a way of changing. The ancient Taoists let us know this perennial truth long ago. For decades I have been aware of this truth, yet it is still so hard for me to open up to; I tend to hold on to things even when they are passé.

A few months ago Arny and I were preparing for an upcoming Worldwork (large-group process) seminar. I was hoping to use some of my new puppets as part of our teaching. However, I couldn't seem to figure out how to do it. Then I began to have a series of dreams that seemed to tell me that I should let the *creative moment* inform my teaching rather than having to produce anything specific. I did not need to use puppets or play music but rather realize that *every moment*, even while teaching, was a potentially creative act. I recalled something I had read about Inayat Khan once again:

> ... Khan felt that he had to give up music in the sense of singing and playing, and from then on he often explained how one should consider life itself as music. All his teachings reveal to us the harmony of the universe, and show the part that each individual, each creature, has to play in this symphony.[2]

The whole concept of creativity began to grow much wider than I had allowed it until that point. Creativity did not belong solely to the realm of materials or art or music but to the whole of life itself. That special *feeling* I have when I play music, the *inspiration* I sense when I create a puppet, the *abandoned moment* of letting a dance come through me was always there, available at any point. In fact, it was this idea that had led me to Process Work in the first place: Process Work focuses on discovering, cherishing, and following the *dreaming process* as it magically presents itself and unfolds throughout the day and night. This dreaming process does not necessarily need a particular medium through which to express itself; *all* media serve equally well. Nevertheless, a particular medium such as a piece of music or a wise puppet can be an initiatory vehicle through which we can get in touch with our dreaming processes.

The point of the book is to tap into the generative flow of the Intentional Field and its constantly creative potential, whether we are working with puppets, going to work, relating with others, or simply walking down the street. My greatest hope is that life becomes more magical for all of us—that we make space for the dreaming to hatch and come to maturity in the fabric of our everyday lives.

Notes

1. Hazrat Inayat Khan, *The Mysticism of Sound and Music* (rev. ed. Boston: Shambhala, 1996), xi.
2. Hazrat Inayat Khan, *The Mysticism of Sound and Music*, vii.

INTRODUCTION
Plant a Seed and It Will Grow

Fava Bean Plant

I was so excited this evening. When we arrived at our house on the Oregon coast after being away for many months, I was thrilled to see that the seeds that I had planted then and simply left in my vegetable garden to fend for themselves actually grew! I yelped and jumped up and down with joy when I saw so many newborn plants reaching upward toward the sky. I really couldn't understand how it all happened; it was a miracle. Ever since I began making a garden about ten years ago, I've been amazed that a tiny seed that looks dried out and lifeless can suddenly spurt up into a green plant full of suppleness and abundance. Admittedly, some of the seeds never made it to the sunlight and, as fate has it, will remain forever under the ground or in the tummy of a bird. Yet other seeds did grow and flower and would soon produce vegetables that we could eat. How could this be?

Arny said that the way I was thinking reminded him of a conversation he'd had with a four-year-old girl who lived next door many years ago. One day the little girl saw Arny planting broccoli and cauliflower seeds. Arny explained that the seeds would grow into plants. Shortly thereafter the little girl began to plant something in an empty patch of earth in her yard. But what did she plant? Arny went over to see what she was doing and discovered that she was planting two of her toys! She assumed that they would also grow! Hey, if a lifeless-looking seed can grow, why not a toy? Arny supported her idea by saying that yes, the toy would grow, but not in the way she expected. It would bloom in her mind. The little girl seemed to understand immediately that the toy would come alive in her mind through fantasies and dreaming.

How I love that story! Every time I think of it I am reminded that there is a life force within everything: an invisible spirit or guide that helps it become its own unique being—whether a plant or teddy bear, person or puppet! The story reminds me that *I* don't have to be the creator; things have their own life force, what we call an *Intentional Field*, that escorts them into their incomparable self. I simply have to be available, open, and surrender to the flow of the Intentional Field as it moves my body, my voice, hands, heart, and mind.

Some days later, after the excitement of seeing my growing plants, I dreamed that I buried a piece of foam, which I had wanted to use to make a puppet, near an apple tree in our garden. In the dream this act had to do with a Native American ritual of some sort. I realized that it was not me who was creating these puppets; instead, they come from the earth, from the native spirit. And when I "plant" them, they will grow in their own natural form, just like the apple tree.

Every time I notice a slight body feeling or glance briefly at a tissue box that catches my attention, I stumble upon a potential seed, which—given enough water and attention—is the beginning of a unique creation. One day I was working in our study and decided to lie back in my chair and take a short nap. Before I dozed off, my sleepy eyes gazed around the room and landed on a book on the bookshelf across the room. I didn't recognize what book it was, and my tired, aging eyes couldn't make out its title. However, some voice inside my weary head said, "Hey, I bet that book can talk!" Almost instantly I began to hear that book recite a poem about how it had been stuck on that bookshelf for a long time and was fed up being neglected and squeezed in between a lot of other similarly bound and paged sisters and brothers for so long! The book had a very nasty and unpleasant temper! His poem began:

> Oh yes, you bet I'm grouchy.
> Wouldn't you be?
> If you were stuck on a shelf
> For a year, or maybe three?

Groucho Gloom

When I got up from my nap, I decided to take that irritable book down and give it some relief. Why not make some space in which it could stretch out and come to life even more? I had a bit of time, so I ran downstairs where I keep all my fabric and art supplies and let *It* manifest further. (Of course, I helped with a little glue and yarn.) The book transformed into a puppet that resembled Groucho Marx in a very bad mood. I called him Groucho Gloom. Groucho's mouth can be opened and closed by putting your hand into a glove wrapped around his binding. When his mouth opens and closes, it makes a *very* obnoxious, snapping sort of sound.

Over time Groucho has become a moody and constant companion, sitting near me at my desk smirking and commenting on just about everything I do! He *always* has something to say – something *negative*, that is! Sometimes he simply depresses me. At other times we've had some really wild and good arguments.

He seemed particularly perturbed by my artwork. He insisted that I make it useful instead of "dilly-dallying," as he called it, in my inner fantasy world. For all of his irksome qualities, and after much resistance on my part, I finally realized that he had a point. I needed to begin to share some of my creative projects with others and to use my puppets and music to augment my teaching. I guess I have to admit that if it weren't for Groucho's prodding, I might never have created this book. Even Groucho conceded that it might be important to open up to "irrational experiences" that we do not

Groucho Gloom

understand at first, to allow them to unfold, and then afterwards
we can always use our conscious minds to sculpt and think about
them. Hey, without doing that, Groucho might have never come
into being!

The Dreaming in Matter

Aboriginal peoples around the world have always known that the
Dreaming lies within matter. The Dreaming exists *prior* to the
material world and gives rise to it. Many of us marginalize the
Dreaming and focus only on the "real" part of things. That's okay
too, but it can be the source of depression or the gnawing feeling
that something is just not quite right, that something is missing in
life, some inspirational spark. The very basis of process-oriented
psychology lies in the idea that this dreaming is *always* there, we
just have to notice its subtle pull and, with a loving focus, allow it
to unfold and enhance our lives. Those things that seem static—
material objects, frustrating body symptoms that do not seem to
change, or unwieldy moods— when approached with wonder and

a Zen-like beginner's mind are found to be processes in the midst of unfolding. This is the Essence of Arny's discovery of the *Dreambody* (i.e., the mirror connection between our dreams and body symptoms) and the dreaming process that is always there day or night.[1]

Even within the most lifeless-looking object or experience lies a wealth of potential. The "real" world that seemed so static a moment ago transmutes into a fluid field of possibilities. This book is based upon finding that beginner's mind and discovering the unfolding and creative force of the Intentional Field inherent in materials, our bodies, sounds, the environment, words, images, and—perhaps most importantly—in our experiences in daily life.

Creativity has always seemed like an enigma to me, and I know there will always be something mysterious about it. It is that mystery that has always pulled, haunted, and excited me. I alternately cherish and fear its hidden dimensions and energy. Yet at the same time, there is another aspect of it that is easy and utterly natural. I think it is our natural inheritance to be creative.

Think of children. Kids are continually creative without even thinking about it. Consider your dreams. You go to sleep and something begins to weave the most magnificent or horrific adventures. That creative storytelling capacity occurs all by itself. Arny says that this creative dreaming process not only happens at night but all day long as well. He calls it the "dreaming process"; most recently he described it as "24-hour lucid dreaming."[2] In order to enter into that ongoing stream of dreaming, simply notice very subtle things that catch your attention, hold on to them, then let them speak to you. Plant them, water them, and let them develop and unfold in their own natural and creative way. Or, if an egg is a more appealing analogy, notice the egg, warm it up, and watch how it hatches! The point is, *we* do not have to *be* creative; creativity is always present. We simply need to tend to our experiences with an openminded and loving awareness.

In fact, why not ask yourself a simple question: "What seed is trying to grow in me just now? What egg is about to hatch?" Ask that question again and again throughout the day, throughout your life, and it will present something new and interesting each time—a new seed beginning to grow, a new egg beginning to hatch.

Working on Yourself with This Book as a Guide

It is my hope that this book will inspire you to experience a new zest for life, to step out of known convention and go beyond even what you have dreamed until now, to see all of life as an invitation for creative potential. I hope this book will show you how creativity is always there—waiting for you to notice at any moment in the "almost nothing" that catches your attention.[3] If you stay close to this murky and magical moment, you will discover the beginning of new and creative worlds.

Throughout these pages you will have the chance to tap into art, music, puppetry, and the creativity of everyday life. You will find stories, anecdotes, pictures, theory, and simple exercises that help you work on yourself and show you how to explore and be moved by the Intentional Field. There are at least three ways to use this book. One is to read it from beginning to end. The second is to open it up to any page whenever you need a suggestion about getting on with your work and read from there. Yet another possibility is to put it by your bedside in case you wake up in the night and need inspiration.

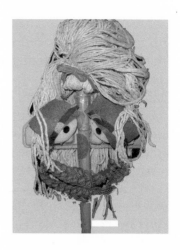

Mop Head

The tone of this book swings with the various moods I went through while writing it. Sometimes the tone is serious, sometimes spiritual, at other times utterly mundane, and often whimsical and lighthearted. As a whole, I chose a very personal writing style to generate an intimate and cozy atmosphere in which you will, hopefully, feel free to explore your own creative impulses and dreams. I also try to incorporate those incessant critics who attack our dreaming and creative work. In fact, you will see that the critics who disturb you and even seem to inhibit your creativity can be seeds for much creative energy. As previously mentioned, some of my best inspiration has come out of some of the most miserable, nagging critics like Groucho Gloom.

I give numerous examples, some from my own experiences and others from some of my class participants and clients. I also intersperse a few short interludes that I just couldn't fit in anywhere else! Some of them address those all too typical and dangerous moments during creative work when we say things like "I'll do it later" or "I don't know the next step." In addition, the quality of the pictures varies in order to mirror the idea that perfectionism and final projects are not the point. Rather the focus is on the spontaneous and creative act of following the path of the Intentional Field.

This book is for anyone who would like to have a rich and artistic life. The methods are also helpful for those of you who are therapists and who would like to bring a creative and artistic dimension to your work with others.

Many people have told me that the hardest thing about creativity is that they do not give themselves the time or space to do it. There is always something else to do! I know this tendency in myself. Sometimes I think that half the work is to simply create a space, an atmosphere to dream—even if it is only for a brief moment. I hope this book will encourage you to take that moment now and then in your daily life—or, if you prefer, take that hour or two. For many people it is helpful to have the support of creating with others. If that is the case for you, try the exercises in this book with a friend or even a group!

The exercises are not set in stone; use them only as guideposts to explore your creative impulses. Some of them require materials; some simply require you! Use whatever materials are easiest and nearest to you. Even a rubber band or a toothpick can be enough.

Or if you prefer, gather more elaborate stuff with which to play. Remember, however, that the point of all the exercises is to get in contact with the Intentional Field behind creative expression.

Harry the Hippie

Oh, dear. One of my puppets is interrupting me just now and telling me that I have to talk about him. His name is Harry the Hippie. Harry is a narcissist who feels that he should always be talking and listened to. He says that I should tell you about the film that he starred in.

Harry the Hippie

Harry is referring to the musical puppet production I created called *What I Want to Be When I Grow Up*. In the very beginning of that show Harry bursts through the back of a bookshelf stuffed with books. (Hmm, I seem to have a thing going with books!) Harry is struggling hard to get through the paperbacks and hardbacks. In an exasperated tone, he says, "Gee, it takes a lot of strength to get through that thing you call 'reality'! Couldn't you make it easier, like make the door a little wider? Huh? Do I have to wait until you go to sleep at night to get through more easily? Gee, I'm exhausted!"

Poor Harry had a good point, and he wants me to stress it again here. He says there is frequently a great tension between the often conflicting worlds of dreaming and reality. I personally have struggled with the realist and the dreamer sides of myself as long as I can remember. Harry says that he comes from the puppet dream world but wants to be known and recognized in the land of ordinary reality. He made me aware that without access to his world of puppets and imagination while living in the everyday world, life might feel one-dimensional, barren, or depressing. He stressed that *both worlds* are important and need one another to have the sense of a full life. I hope this book will be one window into how these worlds can come together and teach us to fly in the midst of everyday existence.

Last night I dreamed that I discovered a huge garden located just next to our house, which I had forgotten about. I was surprised to find that I had planted some beautiful trees there. I then noticed that there were hundreds of other plants in the garden that other people had planted. Many people shared that same garden. I hope that this book is one of the plants that we share in the garden of a creative life.

Amy Mindell
Oregon, 2005

Notes

1. For a history of the developments of these ideas, see Arnold Mindell, "Some History, Theory and Practice Beginning with the Dreambody and Including the Quantum Mind and Healing," article on author's website (http://www.aamindell.net/processwork_frame.htm), 2004.
2. Arnold Mindell, *Dreaming While Awake: Techniques for 24-Hour Lucid Dreaming* (Charlottesville, Virginia: Hampton Roads, 2000), 3-16.
3. Arnold Mindell, *The Shaman's World: Paths of Creation in Psychology, Spirituality, and Physics* (forthcoming), chapter 1.

Part I

SEEDS OF CREATIVITY

Sally

Chapter 1

THE INTENTIONAL FIELD

I don't know where fate will find me
On the road, when darkness fills the air
But I feel you right behind me
Always there
Trees are swaying in the starlight
As the moon flashes everywhere
I'm not alone in the wilderness
You're always there
Always there

(From my song "Always There")

As I embarked on writing this book, I began to research creativity. As I read more and more, it suddenly felt unnecessary to me to add one more book to the pile. At the same time, the process of creativity seemed so individual in nature that saying anything at all might be too general to be of use. I also worried that speaking about it might ruin the elegant mystery of it all. I decided to give up trying.

Then something happened. As I stepped back and let go of my conscious programs, I found myself diving beneath my conflicting thoughts and was soon swimming in a murkier, unknown sea. In this cloudy and blurry state I found myself turning toward something that has been of great significance to me in recent times. In our seminars over the past several years, my partner Arny and I have focused on a force that subtly guides and sets our lives into motion and brings the material world to birth. It is a force akin to the Aboriginal Australian concept of the *Dreaming*, the invisible flow which gives rise to the material world. Arny had called it the *Intentional Field*.[1]

As I dove down even deeper, it dawned on me that the Intentional Field can be understood as the core or seed of the creative process, the mother of all things—an ever-flowing stream that can be stepped into at any time for creative inspiration, whether we are working on a creative project or simply moving through our everyday life.

It's easy to imagine the Intentional Field if you watch the activity of little children; kids are always in its flow without the inhibitions many adults possess. They are simply *moved* from one thing to the next by an imperceptible force. One toy can spark the beginning of a story or scenario that seems to appear out of the blue! Likewise, when I begin to play with foam, there is an almost imperceptible force that moves me and moves the foam, a force that draws both of us into an inexplicably creative act.

I have found that the Intentional Field can become a close friend and ally, a flowing river that can be stepped into at any moment for creative inspiration.

Experiencing the Intentional Field

in Movement

It is difficult to speak in words about the Intentional Field, so before going further, let's first try to sense it experientially. I never like to talk about things too much before experiencing them. Afterwards, we will think more about it theoretically.

This basic exercise focuses on noticing the Intentional Field as it expresses itself through your body. You can do this exercise at any time, night or day, on a bus or sitting in a class (especially if you do the movement part of it in a subtle way!). Steps 1-5 only take a few minutes. If you'd like to unfold your experience further follow steps 6-9 for another 10 minutes. It is easiest to begin the exercise from a sitting position.

Exercise

Materials: A piece of paper. A pen, crayon, or marker with which to draw.

1. Sit in a position that is open to movement; for example, sit at the edge of a chair. Close your eyes and take a few breaths.
2. Now, notice a slight tendency in your body to move in a particular direction, but don't move yet. Just notice the subtle tendency for your body to begin to move in a particular direction. Notice it, without actually moving your body.
3. Now begin to let that tendency slowly move and unfold through your body in space. As you move, notice any images that come up in conjunction with those motions. Trust whatever image emerges even if it doesn't make sense right away. Now imagine a sound that goes with that particular image and motions.
4. If you haven't already, imagine that experience as some kind of figure—human, animal, or some other part of nature. Become this figure by sitting like it, moving like it, and feeling its feelings.

Tendency Dance

5. Allow that experience to unfold further in any way that you like, until it explains itself to you in some way or gives you a message.
6. Now take a piece of paper and your pencil, crayon, or marker and make a quick sketch that expresses that experience. Write a few words or a short poem next to the sketch.
7. Now imagine allowing that experience to express itself even further through some creative modality. For example, imagine what type of puppet might you create from that experience? What type of painting? What photographs would you take to capture that quality? What sort of music, dance, sculpture, or theater piece might emerge based on that experience? What creative teaching style might arise? What sort of relationship style would this experience suggest? Choose a medium that arises naturally from that experience and fantasize about its creative fruits. (At another point, if you feel the urge, go ahead and actually create these things.)
8. Finally ask yourself how this experience might influence and contribute to your everyday life and work.
9. Write down notes about this experience. You might also ask yourself if this experience is connected to a dream that you had recently and how it might help to interpret that dream.

When I did this exercise, my tendency was an ever-so-slight movement of my torso forward. As I followed this movement, I began to slump forward in my chair. As I did this, I had the image of a hobo who had no energy and who was waiting for something to move her. Her message had to do with encouraging me to give up my will, be empty, and let something else inspire and guide me. When I imagined how that experience might manifest in some creative form, I immediately envisioned a puppet made partly out of burlap whose name was Golden Hair. Later that day I created her.

Golden Hair

Golden Hair reminded me that tapping into and following the Intentional Field is something like going through a mini sacrifice or a mini "death." It requires dropping our momentary identity and goals for a brief moment in order to get in contact with the flow of life that is moving us.

More on the Intentional Field

Now that you have had a brief experience of the Intentional Field, let me describe it in greater detail—first in a feeling way, and then in terms of a larger theoretical context.

In the previous exercise we began by noticing a tendency that moves our bodies. You were probably unaware of this subtle tendency before you focused on it, yet this delicate inclination or flow is always there. The Intentional Field guides and organizes our experiences invisibly and immeasurably, even though we are usually unaware of its presence.[2] The subtle experiences of the Intentional Field are there even before we can speak about them. The Taoists might call this force *the Tao that can't be said*, which then manifests and expresses itself in *the ten thousand things* or *the Tao that can be said.*

Originally, the concept of the Intentional Field arose out of Arny's studies of quantum physics and the quantum wave function.[3] The quantum wave function is the basic pattern behind all of matter, but it cannot be seen directly. The Intentional Field is one name Arny used to reinterpret the quantum wave function. He draws on the following analogy to describe the Intentional Field: if you put a magnet under metal filings, it will invisibly begin to organize the filings into a pattern.[4] He likened this invisible guiding force to the physicist David Bohm's concept of a guiding wave, or pilot wave.[5]

Even if you are not a physicist, the indigenous part of you knows that everything is imbued with dreaming, with an unseen force that moves it about. Everything is alive, so to speak, and has a spirit within it.[6] As a Process Work therapist, it has always been my desire to find and support this deep flow that is moving an individual, couple, or group. In our work with dying people, Arny and I have been awed repeatedly by the way in which the Intentional Field, which has always been guiding the individual's life, manifests most clearly just near death.

At this point you might think it strange to call this an Intentional Field. From the perspective of ordinary consciousness, this flow seems unintentional, yet from *its* viewpoint—from the viewpoint of dreaming—it is *intentional* and has a distinct path.

Dimensions of Experience

In order to understand where the Intentional Field fits into a larger framework, let's take a look at a special diagram that Arny developed to illustrate the various dimensions of awareness. You can read about this larger framework in other places,[7] so I'll just sum-marize here.

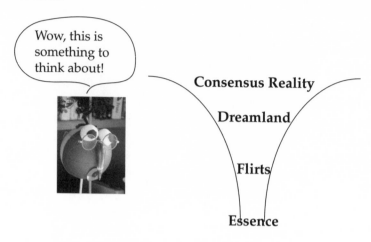

Consensus Reality

Dreamland

Flirts

Essence

Consensus Reality refers to the everyday reality that most people consent upon, the *doings* of our world, the agreed upon names of objects, etc. It also includes the typical way we identify ourselves, which we call *primary processes* in Process Work. The world of Consensus Reality is dualistic, meaning that we can speak of separate parts in relationship to one another.

Dreamland includes dreamlike experiences, figures, and images from our dreams, as well as our subjective experiences. Dreamland is also dualistic in the sense that we can speak about separable parts. It is, however, a *nonconsensual* realm. That is, people will not consent to, or agree upon, its subjective and dreamlike contents for the very reason that those contents are subjective. For example, no one can empirically verify (that is, achieve a consensus on the fact) that I feel as if there is a fiery monster in my stomach when I experience my acid-stomach difficulties!

Flirts are discussed later in this chapter.

The Essence realm is also a nonconsensual level of experience. It is the realm of subtle tendencies that occur *before* they can be ver-balized, such as the *tendency* to move before moving, as we experi-enced in the previous exercise. Experiences here are subtle and fleeting. We often call them *sentient* experiences. It is difficult to speak about this realm, because it points to those experiences that occur prior to verbalization.

Sun on the Ocean

Experiences in the Essence realm are nondualistic in the sense that they cannot be differentiated into parts. Rather, we experience a kind of oneness, a sense that we have touched upon a deep, eternal, or cosmic aspect of ourselves. We sometimes experience this realm spontaneously in deep meditation, during ecstatic states of consciousness, or in near-death experiences.

Essence-level experiences are the seed, root, or egg of an experience that, when unfolded, manifests in dualistic forms and images that we can speak about in Dreamland and Consensus Reality. For example, in the previous movement exercise, my subtle tendency unfolded in terms of a hobo figure in Dreamland. When I create her out of materials and begin to apply her message in my everyday life, I enter the realm of Consensus Reality.

The Essence is called by many names in various cultures and spiritual traditions, such as our *immortal selves, the Dreaming* in Aboriginal cultures, *the Tao that can't be said* in Taoism, and the *Rig Pa* state in Tibetan Buddhism.

The Invisible Force of the Intentional Field

The Essence realm is a name for a *general* region of awareness. The Intentional Field can be understood as the *inherent movement within* the Essence. A helpful analogy is to imagine the Essence represented in the form of the moon and the Intentional Field as the gravitational pull of the moon on the water that creates waves. We cannot see this field, but if we were in a boat on the ocean we would feel its force.

Yet another way to understand the Intentional Field is to envisage it as a *life force* within materials. For example, imagine that the seed of a tree represents the Essence. The life force that flows out of that seed and guides it into its unique tree-form can be understood as the Intentional Field. We can't see this life force (just as we cannot see the force of gravity), but it is there and helps the tree grow into its unique structure.

Tree Overlooking the Ocean

If we are able to use our subtle awareness to notice and unfold the magical flow of the Intentional Field as it arises out of the Essence realm, even before we know what it is about we can discover a great source of creativity. However, much of the time this flow happens unconsciously, without our awareness. In those cases, the Intentional Field can manifest as disturbances in Dreamland and Consensus Reality in such forms as body symptoms or difficult relationship situations. When this occurs, it is still possible to rediscover the Intentional Field within these difficult experiences and find the fluidity and hidden creativity within them. (See Chapter 11 on body symptoms.)

Parallel Worlds

When the Intentional Field arises in Dreamland, it can take many forms. Arny uses a term from physics to describe these various forms as "parallel worlds." (See Part III for more on parallel worlds.) Recall your experience in the previous exercise. The figure or image that arose is one of the parallel worlds arising in you today. If you do this exercise tomorrow or even later today, you might experience a very different parallel world arising. However, in the same way that one individual diamond has many facets, each of your parallel worlds adds up to a basic pattern or story that is guiding you in life.[8] In fact, you can also try a number of different exercises in this book on a particular day and notice how they add up to a basic story in your life. For example, when I did this, the parallel worlds that emerged added up to the figures in my earliest childhood dream.[9]

Additionally, the realms of Consensus Reality, Dreamland, and the Essence can also be understood as parallel worlds for one another; all of them exist simultaneously, though we tend to focus on one realm at any given moment.[10] As Harry the Hippie reminded us in the Introduction, life without access to all of these dimensions can feel depressing.

It is possible to move between these parallel dimensions. For example, you can start at Consensus Reality with a momentary feeling or mood, with an everyday reality problem, or with a body symptom, and then discover the Essence behind that experience. You can begin with a dream image in Dreamland and get to its Essence as well. Or you can start with the Essence and Intentional Field, as we did in the first exercise, and follow that experience as it unravels and emerges into ordinary reality. Throughout the book we will experiment with moving between these levels. Most importantly, we focus on *our fluidity*—our ability to move between these worlds—and on the way in which this fluidity is central to our sense of wellness and creativity.[11]

Flirts

Just above the Essence level is the area of "Flirts." Flirts are the first way in which the Essence world arises in our awareness, the first way that we experience the movement of the Intentional Field.

Flirting Bird

Flirts are quick, evanescent, nonverbal sensations, visual flickers, moods, and hunches that suddenly catch our attention. Such experiences occur very rapidly. For example, our attention might be grabbed for a split second by the brilliant color of a flower or the chirping sound of a bird. Such Flirt-like experiences are of such brief duration that we normally do not stay with them long enough to help them unfold and come into consciousness. They are fleeting and nonconsensual.

The moment we notice a Flirt that has captured our attention, we have caught the tail of a creative process in the midst of unfolding. This is so exciting that I will save it for a longer discussion in Part II.

The Intentional Field:

Medium, Parameters, and Play

Now let's consider a few qualities of the Intentional Field. The Intentional Field that flows from the Essence is invisible and immeasurable, yet we can also catch a glimpse of it through the use of various media. For example, divination procedures like the I Ching use coins or sticks to reveal the momentary path of the Tao or Intentional Field.

So one way to know the Intentional Field is to use a *medium* or *parameter* within which it can show and express itself. In the earlier exercise we used our bodies as a medium by which to discover the pattern of the Intentional Field. Another medium is a sandbox.[12] If you give a child or adult a sandbox, the Intentional Field that was previously in the background emerges spontaneously.

Using a few materials to get in touch with the flow of the Intentional Field is an easy way to begin. I had a funny experience of this in one of my classes. I came into the room with a bunch of materials that I hoped to use in an exercise later in the class, an exercise that would help us experience the Intentional Field. As we waited a few minutes before beginning the class, I was amazed to see most of the participants spontaneously grabbing and playing with the materials I had brought. They even started to create all kinds of things with them—costumes, impromptu puppets, hats, etc. I started to laugh and realized that I could forget the exercise I had planned—contact with the flow of the Intentional Field had already begun!

Each of us has our own medium through which we connect to the Intentional Field. Some people like paints, others toys, some puppets, others writing, some relationships, some cooking, others like to daydream and catch their fantasies. What are your preferred methods? Are there some that you go back to again and again? I often simply sit with all my material around me and see what "catches fire."

Some people use music and specific parameters as their preferred method. Musician and composer John Zorn says,

> For me, composition is problem solving. I try to go to new places by setting myself parameters and trying to solve the problems they present. How can I create a piece that has only three sounds in it?[13]

A most important metaskill or feeling attitude when investigating the Intentional Field is that of play. Simply take materials and begin to play with them, and see what emerges. In his book on animation, Kit Laybourne says that "insight and creativity happen when one is playing around."[14] The Nobel prize-winning physicist Richard Feynman says that you have to play and not worry about the outcome or ascribe any purpose to what you are doing:

> I used to *enjoy* doing physics. Why did I enjoy it? I used to *play* with it. I used to do whatever I felt like doing—it didn't have to do with whether it was important for the development of

nuclear physics, but whether it was interesting and amusing for me to play with.[15]

So, why not grab three objects that are around you just now. Any three. Start to play with them, and you will notice that you begin to create something. What did you create, build, or sculpt? Each person will come up with something different. *Voila!* You've discovered the flow of the Intentional Field that is invisibly, yet powerfully, moving you.

Losing Track of the Flow

I hope that this book will help us get in touch with the Intentional Field as a lifestyle, whether it involves creating something artistically, enriching a walk down the street, deepening our business tasks or our relationship interactions. I must admit, however, that I often forget to notice it. How many times have I forgotten it all and just sort of *did* life? I hold on to my identity and refuse to let go. Or I get fastened to a particular creative product and begin to work hard and forget about the Essence from which it came. Sometimes this attitude results in my feeling moody or exhausted. (See Part IV on critics and blocks for some ideas about how to deal with these types of mood.) Perhaps this is a natural course of events: forgetting or ignoring our subtle experiences until we are so fed up that we have to let go and trust in the wisdom of the unknown, the silent river that is moving us.

Deep in the night, when there's no place to hide
I'll find a river, deep inside
And all my dreams
will start to flow
And down the river
I will go

(from my song "Deep in the Night")

Notes

1. For a detailed discussion of the Intentional Field and the tendencies which arise from it., see Arnold Mindell, *The Quantum Mind and Healing: How to Listen and Respond to Your Body's Symptoms* (Charlottesville, Virginia: Hampton Roads, 2004), 3-14 and 26. His concept of the "force of silence" also arises from that field.
2. Arnold Mindell, *Dreaming While Awake: Techniques for 24-Hour Lucid Dreaming* (Charlottesville, Virginia: Hampton Roads, 2000); *Quantum Mind: The Edge between Physics and Psychology* (Portland, Oregon: Lao Tse Press, 2000).
3. Arnold Mindell, *Quantum Mind*, 165-251; *Dreaming While Awake*, 8-10.
4. Arnold Mindell, *Quantum Mind*, 268-272.
5. For a discussion about Bohm's pilot wave, see Arnold Mindell, *Quantum Mind in Healing*, 69–79.
6. See Phelim McDermott and Julian Crouch. "Puppetry: A User's Guide." (http://www.improbable.co.uk/article.asp?article_id=3). In this lovely article about their use of puppets in their theater productions, Phelim McDermott and Julian Crouch speak about the way in which each piece of scenery is alive. For example, a bed can be moved in such a way as to show that it is shy, bold, fearful, etc.
7. Arnold Mindell, *Dreaming While Awake*, chapters 1-2.
8. For more on parallel worlds, see Arnold Mindell, *Quantum Mind*, 227-236.
9. In Process Work early and repeating childhood dreams or earliest childhood memories are understood as lifelong mythic patterns.
10. Amy Mindell, "Amy's Hyperspaces: Creativity, the Bird of Paradise, and the Doorway to Parallel Worlds" (Article on author's website http://www.aamindell.net/research_frame.htm, 2002).
11. Arny calls this openness to the various realms and parts of ourselves and our groups and communities *Deep Democracy*. See Arnold Mindell, *The Leader as Martial Artist: An Introduction to Deep Democracy Techniques and Strategies for Resolving Conflict and Creating Community*. (San Francisco: HarperCollins, 1992. Reprint. Portland, Oregon: Lao Tse Press, 2000); *Sitting in the Fire: Large Group Transformation through Diversity and Conflict* (Portland, Oregon: Lao Tse Press, 1995); *The Deep Democracy of Open Forums* (Charlottesville, Virginia: Hampton Roads, 2002).
12. See Dora Kalff, *Sandplay: A Psychotherapeutic Approach to the Psyche* (Santa Monica, California: Sigo Press, 1980).
13. Ann McCutchan's *The Muse that Sings: Composers Speak about the Creative Process* (New York: Oxford University Press, 1999), 164.
14. Ann McCutchan's *The Muse that Sings*, 14.

15. Richard Feynman, "The Dignified Professor." In *Creators on Creating: Awakening and Cultivating the Imaginative Mind*, edited by Frank Barron, Alfonso Montuori, and Anthea Barron (New York: Jeremy Tarcher/Putnam, 1977), 66.

Chapter 2

THE ESSENCE OF IT ALL

Lava Rock Tide Pools

T he Essence is like the earth that is always there for us, yet whose presence we do not always pay attention to. It is like a seed from which the plants grow, the origin of the Intentional Field, and the mother of manifest things.

The Essence and Art

When I was creating my musical puppet theater in which all of the puppets speak about their deepest longings and what they want to be when they grow up, an Essence figure arose who wanted to be "The Mother of Our Country." She represents the loving earth and sings:

I'll be a home to the courageous
And the ones who run scared
I'll be a home to the animals
From the mountains to the air
I'll be the mother of our country
From the mountains to the seas
The earth that we walk on
that allows us to be.

She embodies the nondualistic world that is beneath the polarities of Consensus Reality and Dreamland, the common ground that we share. This common ground, "the Tao that can't be said," can be difficult to formulate. Yet when I sing or listen to that song, I feel I am able to connect with this open and generative wellspring.

Just as the Essence goes by various names in psychology and religion, such as *spirit*, *oneness*, and *the transpersonal*, I have been excited to discover that it is also described in a variety of art forms. In the next pages I'd like to share a few of these artistic Essence descriptions with you that I have been studying. At the end of this chapter, I mention a few practical methods aimed at getting to the deep Essence behind our experiences; later we will apply these methods in some of the exercises.

The Ideograph

When Arny and I and two of our friends recently went to see the play *The Lion King* in a theater in London, I think my world started over. *The Lion King* begins with the convergence of African animals to Pride Rock to see the newborn Simba. As the play began, tears burst immediately out of my eyes and flowed uncontrollably down my face for the next ten minutes. From the very start the entire theater filled with actors in colorful costumes, with beautiful rhythms and chanted songs and dances, with multihued masks, and with colorful animal figures of every size (some small and some much larger than life). As the animals continually entered the room, it was at once a flowing menagerie clad in brightly swirling colors, a whirling dance, a community ritual, a joyous choir, and a cacophony of sounds and symphony. It was all so real and so unreal at the same time. How I hoped it would never end! One journalist described the staging as giving the audience "delicious chills."[1] I agree!

Lion with Outstretched Arm

"This is what life is about!" I exclaimed inside my trembling body. All my life I have been yearning for such an experience: an amassing of impressions and music and color and animals that step out of the dreaming and can be seen and felt. How I longed to create this kind of experience one day! Needless to say, I was up all night hearing chants, visualizing colorful costumes, and choreographing dances in my mind for a theater piece I was working on. I recall the gazelles: eight or nine of them mounted on top of wheels that were pushed by an almost invisible, yet visibly human, being. The gazelles' motions astounded me; they leaped in fluid arches, as if in slow motion, hauntingly graceful and alive. The giant giraffes pranced gracefully across the stage and then bent their infinitely long painted necks into the audience. It took me some time to realize that there were humans peering out of those costumes as well. The sun rose in the background: a simple huge circle blazing with orange and yellow light.

In the midst of it all I suddenly remembered something I had read by chance a couple of months earlier. It was an interview with the director, costume designer, mask and puppet maker of *The Lion King*, Julie Taymor. She spoke about a concept she draws upon for all of her works: the ideograph. She describes the ideograph as "an Essence, an abstraction. It's boiling it right down to the most essential two, three brush strokes."[2]

Here was the Essence again. The ideograph mirrored the concept of the Essence as a fundamental and nondual core of an experience—or in this case, of a theater piece. Taymor chose the circle, the circle of life, as the simple yet powerful ideograph for *The Lion King*. She repeated this ideograph in numerous ways throughout the play by creating it as part of the costumes, puppets, masks, and set design.

> You had the sun, then you had the first puppet I conceived, the Gazelle Wheel... this little Gazelle Wheel is the circle of life. So then over and over again, with the audience conscious or not, I'm reinforcing this idea of the wheel.[3]

The ideograph can be particularly important and helpful in terms of creating masks. Although fixed in nature, masks must capture the range, complexity, emotions, and story of a given figure.[4] Taymor asks the actors to find the ideograph of a particular character and to let the character evolve from that basic Essence.

Asian Painting, Haiku, Musical Motifs, and Animation

I was excited to read more about Taymor's understanding of an ideograph as two or three brushstrokes:

> Ideographs are like Japanese brush paintings; one has to abstract the Essence of the image into a few brushstrokes. Detail can be a distraction from the heart of the image.... In ideograph- ing the gestures for each of the figures and eliminating extrane- ous movement, I looked for what was the most minimal action to express the Essence of the moment in time.[5]

I love this minimalist attitude toward getting to the Essence of an experience. During my studies of Asian painting some years ago, I learned about the importance of using only a few brush- strokes to capture the Essence of a subject. I recall the opportunity to watch Zen Master Keido Fukushima Roshi from the Tofukuji monastery in Kyoto demonstrating calligraphy.[6] He meditated in utmost stillness, then suddenly he made a few brushstrokes on his paper. Then it was finished. Similarly, Japanese haiku poems cap- ture the Essence in a mere six lines.

In his lectures on classical music, Professor Robert Greenberg from the San Francisco Conservatory of Music talks about a similar concept in terms of the "musical motif." A musical motif is the building block of melody that contains three or four pitches, upon which the composer then amplifies and builds through "repetition, sequence, and transformation."[7] Just a few pitches create the build- ing blocks from which a composition springs.

Consider one of Greenberg's examples. Most everyone knows Beethoven's Fifth Symphony, which he composed in 1805. Do you remember its compelling beginning? "DA, DA, DA, DAAA!" Just four pitches! Now, try to recall how the music continues. Listen to it internally. (Or if you can't remember, listen to a CD of this music or listen to it on the Web.)

Isn't that amazing? Do you notice how that simple four-note motif repeats and repeats in ever-changing ways? Beethoven soared with those four pitches, creating beautiful patterns and sequences that have survived two centuries. Hearing the begin- ning of this symphony unfailingly makes my heart skip a beat!

Beethoven was able to express the Intentional Field through those few parameters, just a few notes that created one of the most amazing symphonies ever written. I never realized the simplicity of such a motif, the way in which the entire piece springs from it, until Greenberg pointed it out to me.[8]

In a similar vein, I like to think about the art of animation. Animation figures are close to the Essence, for me, because the drawings simplify the subject to a bare minimum in order to capture the absolute core or Essence. In fact, animated figures often seem even more real than the original figure that they are portraying because they bring out the figure's most fundamental qualities. A Disney animator wrote, "Our business is to present something in an unreal way to make it seem more real." [9] Dan McManus, an animated-effects veteran, said, "If you make a pillar of flame the way it really is, it wouldn't look like the real thing. We have to create it as the eye thinks it should look."[10] For example, lightening would not be portrayed just as a bolt in the sky to be effective, but rather the Essence of lightening might be portrayed as sudden staccato bursts of brightness in a dark sky and a crash of sound.

Goddess

Michael Chekhov and the
Psychological Gesture

Thanks to the recommendations of some of my friends, I was thrilled to discover the concept of the Essence beautifully expressed in the work of actor and director Michael Chekhov, the nephew of Anton Chekhov.[11] Chekhov developed and taught actors what he called the *psychological gesture*, which is

> the embodied Essence of the character, a transforming and liberating principle of being which awakes the character into instant and complete life, and which then proliferates into a thousand details which spontaneously and harmoniously evolve.[12]

Chekhov uses remarkably similar terms to describe the Essence as a seed from which an experience arises:

> In a parallel characteristically drawn from the natural world, [Chekhov] believed that a character was like a seed which contained the whole future life of the plant within it. If you grasped one phrase, one gesture, of the character you had access to all the rest; everything would fall harmoniously into place.[13]

The psychological gesture must have a definite and clear form. It "reveals to you the entire character in condensed form, making you the possessor and master of its unchangeable core."[14]

Echoing the sense of simplicity found in the ideograph and musical motifs, the psychological gesture (or PG) should

> be as *simple* as possible, because its task is to summarize the intricate psychology of a character in an easily surveyable form, to compress it into its Essence. A complicated PG cannot possibly do so. A true PG will resemble the broad charcoal stroke on an artist's canvas before he starts on the details.[15]

Chekhov, Beethoven, Taymor, Fukushima Roshi, and so many others speak about the simplicity of the Essence, the generative, unchangeable core of our experiences. The Essence is a source of great creativity. As Chekhov notes, the psychological gesture "proliferates into a thousand details which spontaneously and harmoniously evolve."[16]

Getting to the Essence

In this book I draw on various methods to explore the Essence realm of our experiences. The Essence is almost inexpressible, and therefore it can be helpful to attempt to express it in the form of brief drawings, poetry, gestures, and musical phrases.

Let me mention a few of the methods we will use in this book to find and explore the Essence realm.

Starting with the Essence

In the exercise in Chapter 1, we began by focusing on the Essence level by sitting still and noticing the tendencies toward subtle movements in our bodies. Then we gave room for the Intentional Field to unfold itself further in Dreamland and Consensus Reality first through our bodies and then further, in terms of images, sounds, and words. Finally, we asked ourselves how this experience might be useful in everyday life.

Starting with Experiences in Dreamland or Consensus Reality

You can also start with any experience you are having in Consensus Reality or Dreamland and get to its Essence by finding the seed or core of that experience. To do this, the following two approaches are helpful.

Slow Movement. This method relies on our ability to express an experience we are having in terms of a movement, and then slow that movement down to such a degree that we feel the very first impulse—the initial seed or core—from which that motion emerged. Once this is found, the Essence is often experienced as a piece of nature, such as a rock, a river, a cave.

For example, while working on this manuscript, I noticed that a critical figure inside of me doubted what I was doing. I decided to step into this figure and become it with my body. I stood very straight and made a pointing motion with my right arm and right index finger.

Then I tried to get to the Essence of that critic. Here's how. Still feeling the intensity of the motion, I made the movement once again, but this time slower. Then I made the motion yet again, even more slowly than I had before. I tried it again even slower, still feeling its intensity, until I was barely moving at all; I was just making the very beginning of that movement. At that point, the motion consisted of a very short, quick movement of my right index finger. This motion expressed to me a very exact and pointed attention. This was the very root or Essence of that critic, before he became so big and bad and mean! I went further and imagined this energy as a figure and immediately saw a Zen master who is very exact and aware. I realized that I needed the energy of this Zen master to be very pointed and exact in order to focus and get my work done!

My Puppet Zen Master

Micromovements. Here is a second method to get to the Essence of an experience via Dreamland or Consensus Reality. You can begin with any experience you are having; here we will begin with a body symptom. Imagine you have a pain in your stomach. It feels like a cramp. You express this cramp with your hand, making a tight fist and shaking it in front of you, realizing that you are upset about a few things. This alone can be very helpful and relieving. Perhaps you didn't like something someone said to you during the day, and you need to tell them that.

That's great; but now, let's get to the Essence of that tight fist. Take a moment to relax and put your arms down to your sides.

While relaxed, simply recall the feeling and motion of your fist. Now begin *ever so slightly to recreate* that fist motion, but only move *using the smallest micro-movement of your muscles* in the direction of recreating the fist. As you do that, catch the very first flickering feeling or image or sensation that comes to you. That first flickering sensation is the Essence. You can then make an image of that Essence.

When I did the micro-movement, I felt my muscles pulling in slightly. The very first flickering feeling was one of going deeply inside myself and feeling very steady and solid within. When I made an image out of this Essence, it was a rock that is just there, immovable and centered. At least, that's what happened for me.

How do you know when you have really gotten to the Essence? You know because the experience you have will be nondual in the sense that there won't be questions about it or inner forces in opposition to it. You will be at a core level of experience in which there is only this oneness. For that moment all other polarities or oppositional forces disappear. If you notice that there is still doubt or conflict about your experience, go back and do the movement even more slowly, or make the micromovements even finer, and try once more to sense the very first experience. Trust your intuition. The very quick, subtle experiences that flicker in your attention are most likely the Essence, the "earth" from which your experiences arise.

Now that you have a sense of the Essence, let's turn toward the way in which the Essence and the Intentional Field express themselves in Flirts and materials.

Notes

1. Christine Dolen, "Queen of the Jungle," *Miami Herald Tribune* (20 October 2002).
2. Richard Schechner, "Julie Taymor: From Jacques Lecoq to *The Lion King*," interview with Julie Taymor in *Puppets, Masks and Performing Objects*, ed. John Bell, (Cambridge, Massachusetts: MIT Press, 2001), 28.
3. Schechner, 32.
4. Eileen Blumenthal and Julie Taymor, *Playing with Fire* (rev. ed. New York: Harry Abrams, 1999), 216.
5. Eileen Blumenthal and Julie Taymor, *Playing with Fire*, 82.
6. For examples of Fukushima Roshi's calligraphy, see Jason Wirth, *Zen No Sho: The Calligraphy of Fukushima Keido Roshi* (Santa Fe, New Mexico: Clear Light Books, 2003).
7. Robert Greenberg, "Lecture 8: Style Features of Baroque Music and a Brief Tutorial on Pitch, Motive, Melody, and Texture," *How to Listen to and Understand Great Music* (The Teaching Company, 1998. Audiocassette.)
8. Julie Taymor also likens the ideograph to a musical motif. See Schechner, 29.
9. Bob Thomas, *Disney's Art of Animation: From Mickey Mouse to Beauty and the Beast* (New York: Hyperion, 1991), 74.
10. Thomas, 74.
11. Thanks to the actor and director Phelim McDermott for guiding me to Chekhov's work and its connections with Process Work, theater professor Franc Chamberlain for his insights about Chekhov and his book *Michael Chekhov*, and Arlene Audergon for her article "Process Acting" in *The Journal of Process Oriented Psychology*.
12. Simon Calloway, in his foreword to Michael Chekhov, *To the Actor: On the Technique of Acting* (London: Routledge, 2002), xx.
13. Calloway, xix–xx.
14. Michael Chekhov, *To the Actor: On the Technique of Acting* (London: Routledge, 2002), 68.
15. Chekhov, 71.
16. Chekhov, xx.

DREAMING WHILE I'M AWAKE

Dreambody

I 've always tried to find ways to express my dreaming experiences in everyday life.[1] For those who are interested, here is a little background about some of the creative, dreamlike endeavors that have preoccupied and fascinated me over the years.

Childhood

As a child I was *always* creating something, from knitted scarves to drawings, from watercolor paintings to poems, from clay sculptures to unwieldy cakes. I also spent as much time as possible listening to my favorite music, playing guitar, piano, and a dulcimer that my father bought me in the Appalachian Smoky Mountains. I sang and sang and—well, sang some more. I danced in our backyard, singing loudly as I swung around trees, hoping that a talent scout would just happen to be in the neighborhood and discover me!

As long as I can remember I have been plagued by the split between reality and fantasy, and have felt an urgent need to bring these worlds more closely together. Without access to other dimensions of experience, life feels empty and barren to me. While in a creative madness last summer, I even dreamed that dreaming was a basic *civil right*.

As a kid, nothing could convince me that I couldn't fly. That's why, when I was riding my bike one day along the driveway of a friend's apartment, I decided to speed up instead of stop when I saw that the cement pavement suddenly dropped straight down about four feet to the next driveway below. I decided to go for it, convinced that I could jump with my bike in the air and land on my two wheels. It cost me a lot of blood and skin off my chin, but it was worth it to see if I could do it.

I always loved to dance. In an early memory, of when I was about five years old, I remember twisting to a rock-and-roll tune in our living room. I enjoyed it so much that my parents thought I would twist myself right into the ground! I took lessons in ballet, tap, toe, and jazz. Arny and I still laugh at some of the hilarious pictures of me dancing in silly costumes with my limbs flying in the air—autonomous, miscellaneous limbs jiggling and flying in all directions! Over the years I took many dance lessons and performed with my dance school, acted in many original plays in high school, as well as co-wrote and choreographed one of them.

Me, Dancing as a Young Girl

Though I never considered myself a very good artist, I went through a bunch of art phases. In junior high school I went through a *hands* phase. I'll never forget the day that my art teacher held up one of my pictures to the class and asked with a humorous edge, "Guess who made this?" Everyone started to laugh because everything, and I mean *everything*, I made at that time involved *hands* in one form or another. I'll always remember my brown speckled ceramic pot that was held up by two clay hands. The wrists of the hands formed the base of the pot. To this day it still escapes me why I had such a *hands* thing!

Sugar Cube Castles

This afternoon while making a rare cup of espresso, I caught myself staring briefly at a sugar cube. I giggled at this Flirtlike experience and was suddenly flooded with a memory long forgotten. I was thrown back to a day in elementary school when we were given a homework assignment: to express, through some type of artwork, one of the historical events we were studying in class.

I remember gathering cardboard, glue, and sugar cubes. I embarked on the creation of a huge castle (at least, it seemed huge to me at the time). The castle had four sturdy sugar-cube walls that, once my father helped me spray paint them silver, looked like piled up stone pillars. There was an empty courtyard inside and an opening in the front where the gate would normally be. I placed a female doll on a plastic horse and thereby completed my vision of Helen conquering the city of Troy. I remember feeling indescribably satisfied as I relived history, as I saw it, through my sugar-cube world and Helen's triumph.

College

I studied dance and theater in college. Many of my college days were spent in those departments practicing, training, choreographing, and performing. I had a wonderful teacher, Dimi Reber, and choreographed both serious and amusing dances (for myself and to perform with others) about nature, magic, sports, and the beauty of movement. I also participated in a group that developed and performed educational dance programs for elementary school children. These years provided a special opportunity to discover and share some of my deepest feelings and dreams with a wider community.

Zurich

When I went to Zurich in 1980 and joined the Process Work community, I began to work on and learn more deeply about myself. I was thrilled to discover Process Work's fundamental embrace of the importance of living the Dreaming in daily life. When I became a therapist, I was delighted to be able to experience the co-mingling flow of reality and dreaming with my clients. I have incorporated many of my creative leanings into my practice and teaching, using sound, painting, movement, toys, and puppets to deepen and enrich this aspect of my creative work.

While in Zurich I was also possessed with the desire to express my own dreaming process in some artistic and material form. I did a good deal of painting and drawing (such as the Dreambody painting at the beginning of this chapter) and created miniature shoes out of baked dough: running shoes, hiking boots, ice skates, whatever!

Dough Shoes

My Wood-and-Stone Room (photo and drawing)

Soft Sculptures

I also began to make miniatures of everything from wooden dolls to wooden rocking chairs. I still have a picture of a little room I created in which there was a wooden rocking chair, stone walls, a couple of wooden-framed windows, a knitted oval rug, and a basket filled with knitting supplies. I guess I was creating a cozy home that I was searching for inside myself.

I then turned to soft sculpture, creating picture frames out of satin material with stuffed and sculpted pantyhose people inside.

While in Zurich my enchantment with music continued. A friend and I panhandled for money on the streets by strumming and singing songs from the 1960s and '70s, together with a guy we met who played upright bass.[2] We tried to bring the streets of central Switzerland alive with the tunes of Simon and Garfunkel, Bonnie Raitt, and James Taylor. We made some money—mostly, I think, because the crowd liked hearing music from the U.S. at that time. At least we earned enough to treat ourselves afterward to a Coupe Denmark, that delicious version of a Swiss hot-fudge sundae, that I greedily devoured long before I knew anything about cholesterol! Ah... the good ol' days!

Oh, yes, music. I have already spoken about the way in which songwriting began to pour out of me when I turned forty. I think I had been waiting for the opportunity to write music my whole life, as music has always spoken to my deepest feelings about life. It felt as though I had opened a door that had been locked for decades. When the door opened, out of it flowed sounds, notes, melodies, lines, and feelings. The night was music's time in which I could release myself enough to let it flow, composing a mélange of classical-sounding pieces, folk songs, children's songs, and musical theater compositions. I felt that music conveyed the world of my dreaming more than anything else. In my song "Heaven Is Open," I say:

Dreams are like a rainbow, they can paint the sky
Oh where will they take me, when they fly?

Portland and Creating Together

When Arny and I moved back to the States in the early 1990s, I found myself developing classes about creativity. Together with a friend, I gave a class at the Process Work Center of Portland in which we experimented with all kinds of creative exercises.[3] I'll never forget the day we drew full-length outlines of our bodies on paper. A very dear woman who had cancer at the time took her drawing home and proceeded to fill her body outline with pansies. The picture exquisitely portrayed the gentle yet colorful aspects of her natural self.

During that class, I became interested in recycling materials that I found around the house, and I began to make braided baskets out of the shiny colored advertisement sections of newspapers.

Woven Newspaper Baskets

Shortly thereafter I began to create foam puppets; I was thrilled from morning till night. I ordered a wonderful book, *The Foam Book*, by Allison and Devet that described some of the methods of the craft. I was instantly submerged in an unwieldy world of foam bits and pieces, stretchy, furry, and colorful materials, hot glue, pins and tape, and assorted eyeballs! As I smooshed and twisted the foam, sudden screeches and gasps blurted out of my lips as unusual faces and funny expressions appeared in what was once seemingly lifeless material.

Later on, I developed another series of creativity classes based on following the Intentional Field and how *it* blooms and creates through various materials. This book contains many of the insights and exercises from those classes. In one series of classes, which I taught together with a friend, we explored the Intentional Field as it arose in puppets and masks, and through our bodies and voices.[4] I relished and thrived in the atmosphere of creating together with others. Gathering together seemed to be an important support for many in their creative endeavors as well.

Silly Milly and the Vitamins

Most recently I created a musical puppet theater called *What I Want to Be When I Grow Up*, starring my homemade puppets Silly Milly and the Vitamins. I think this was the most satisfying project I have ever done, because I was able to bring together many of my interests into one unified and entertaining event. During our vacation time I spent every hour of the day and many hours of the night consumed by the creation of puppets, filming, composing and recording songs in a range of styles (from country western to rock and roll, from classical music to folk tunes), and editing all of the video and sound into one package. I think I was more possessed by this project than any other in my life. I imagine that during that time I must have looked like the face in the amazing painting that two of my friends made for me when I completed that project (see below).[5] On the painting itself, my friends wrote many of the words of the songs from that "Silly Milly" production!

Well, that's a little about some of my creative wanderings thus far. Now let's turn to the next section about Flirts and the life of materials.

Silly Milly Painting by Randee and Jan

Notes

1. The title for this chapter comes from Arnold Mindell, *Dreaming While Awake: Techniques for 24-Hour Lucid Dreaming* (Charlottesville, Virginia: Hampton Roads, 2000).
2. Thanks to Dawn Menken for playing music with me.
3. Thanks to Jytte Vikkelsoe for experimenting with me.
4. Thanks to Rhea for creating one of these classes with me.
5. Thanks to Randee Levine and Jan Dworkin for their great painting.

Part II

FLIRTS AND THE
LIFE OF MATERIALS

King Leaf

Chapter 3

FLIRTS AND THE LAND OF MURK AND MAGIC

From Garbage to Gold

L et's focus now on one of the most mysterious and awesome sources of creativity: that moment when the Intentional Field begins to bubble up and express itself as an evanescent, flickering Flirt that catches our attention.

Flirts come in many forms (actually, they can come in *any* form) and can be terrific food for creativity. Every time something Flirts with you—every time something suddenly catches your attention—whether it is a leaf blowing gently in the wind or the sound of the spinning wheels of a car, it is a seed that has a life force within it, an Intentional Field that is just beginning to bloom. A Flirt can be anything from the sound of a creaking floor to a sudden flash of light, to the most banal stuff, such as the dirt on the side of a garbage can or the whizzing sound of a bee racing past your nose! Catching and unfolding these experiences and letting them bloom in creative form is the ultimate in recycling. Even a flickering inner criticism that pops up and catches your attention is a seed that can generate a great deal of creativity.

The composer Igor Stravinsky comments on the importance of observing Flirts, or, in his terms, "the commonest and humblest thing, items worthy of note":[1]

> The faculty of creating is never given to us all by itself. It always goes hand in hand with the gift of observation. And the true creator may be recognized by his ability always to find about him, in the commonest and humblest thing, items worthy of note. He does not have to concern himself with a beautiful landscape; he does not need to surround himself with rare and precious objects. He does not have to put forth in search of discoveries: they are always within his reach. He will have only to cast a glance about him. Familiar things, things that are everywhere, attract his attention. The least accident holds his interest and guides his operations. If his finger slips, he will notice it; on occasion, he may draw profit from something unforeseen that a momentary lapse reveals to him.[1]

---

1. Reprinted by permission of the publisher from *Poetics of Music in the Form of Six Lessons* by Igor Stravinsky, translated by Arthur Knodel and Ingolf Dahl, pp. 54-55, 63-64, Cambridge, Mass.: Harvard University Press, Copyright (c) 1942, 1947, 1970, 1975 by the President and Fellows of Harvard College.

I recently saw a wonderful film about the puppeteer Basil Milovsoroff.[2] His puppets impressed me greatly because many of them were made from pieces of wood that he found in the forest near his home in Vermont. The creations, which emerged out of those pieces of wood, were magnificently brought to life through Milovsoroff's artistic abilities. Everyone knows what it is like to look at a blank wall or at a branch of tree that has fallen or a piece of driftwood and suddenly see a creature emerge. A darkened indentation looks like an eye, the many pieces of bark sticking up look like hair or a mouth jutting upward. It's all there at any moment, waiting to come to life! For example, look very briefly at the picture on page 53 of tree bark that we found near our house on the Oregon coast. What caught your attention? What did you see or imagine? You might have seen a bird, a fan, a face, or who knows what! Many remember doing this as a child—staring at the clouds and seeing funny faces or animals or witches flying in the sky. Catching Flirts is really a very natural, everyday occurrence, though we almost never focus on it in detail.

Leonardo da Vinci also suggested that inspiration and marvelous ideas lie in the most mundane or common places, such as the stains of walls, ashes of a fire, the shape of clouds, or the patterns in mud. According to his notebooks, da Vinci would sometimes throw a paint-filled sponge against the wall and contemplate the stains.[3]

Foggy, Creative Mind, and Lucidity

If you would like to cultivate your ability to catch Flirts, it is most helpful to acquire the metaskill of a *cloudy* or *foggy mind*; one that is unfocused and open, similar to an empty mind or a beginner's mind in Zen Buddhism. Zen master Keido Fukushima Roshi, head abbot of the Tofukuji Monastery of Kyoto, prefers the translation "creative mind," which suggests that the mind is not simply empty but full of creative potential.[4] Shunryu Suzuki writes about this state of mind:

> If your mind is empty, it is always ready for anything; it is open to everything. In the beginner's mind there are many possibilities; in the expert's mind there are few.[5]

I love the following story about Thomas Edison that illustrates the importance of an empty/creative mind:

> Whenever [Thomas Edison] interviewed a job applicant, he would invite them to lunch and order the applicant a bowl of soup. If the applicant seasoned his or her soup before tasting it, he would not hire the applicant. He felt the applicant had so many built-in assumptions about everyday life that it would take too much time to train the applicant to think creatively.[6]

Another aspect of this empty/creative mind is that it does not have preconceptions about what something is about, but rather assumes the attitude of a student who is open to the spontaneous changes of the Tao, without knowing ahead of time what will occur. This mind is "simple" and holds the world in wonder.[7] The songwriter and performer Rickie Lee Jones speaks about this creative process:

> It really is a spirit being born. It's a living spirit.... And you have to be really quiet and careful with it when it's first being born, and you can't tell it it's wrong, cause it will just die.[8]

How difficult this is to do! Many of us try to be intelligent and to guess what something is about before it has a chance to hatch! The creative mind, on the other hand, flows in the opposite direction. It focuses on letting go, emptying the mind, entering the murky and magical realm, and being open to an unknown mystery that is about to unfold.

Actually, the kind of foggy mind that I am describing has a special kind of awareness attached to it, a subtle kind of attention called *lucidity.*[9] Lucid awareness is the ability to be foggy and open, and at the same time to notice the slightest events that catch our attention, those tiny sparks that we often marginalize with our ordinary consciousness. Now there's a paradox for you! You have to be open enough to empty your mind and at the same time notice things that only slightly flicker!

Using lucid attention to catch and hold a Flirt can be very helpful during those moments when you have worked really hard and applied yourself to a task but have not come up with a satisfactory solution to your work. At this disagreeable and frustrating moment, it can be helpful to let go, to allow your lucid, foggy mind

Harold Sees the Light

to emerge, and to notice the tiny things that Flirt with your attention. Once you catch this Flirt, you can then meditate upon its significance in respect to the larger context of your work. Many scientists and artists speak about dropping their work for a while, doing something entirely different such as washing the dishes or going to sleep, and then suddenly a spontaneous revelation appears.

There is one other metaskill that is important for this creative process. After using your lucid attention to notice something that Flirts with you, the metaskill of love or compassion is important to hold; you need to embrace and make a space in which that fleeting experience can unfold. Think of a mother hen who sits on her egg until it hatches. Only with such attention will the experience begin to emerge. Perhaps another word for this metaskill is *devotion*: the practice of lucid attention requires a devotion to those things that nature brings to us and with which we seek intimate contact.

From Mush to Form:
Flowing through the Dimensions

Let's think a bit more about what happens when the mother hen sits on her egg and it begins to warm and grow.

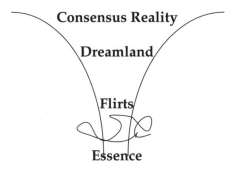

When the Intentional Field begins to rise out of the Essence, a murky area first emerges in which we sense something but do not quite know yet what it is. Will it be a chicken, a baby, a puppet, or a painting? This is magical, awesome, and sometimes frustrating territory. For me, lingering and wading in this *murky realm of becoming*, from which something new is beginning to emerge, is one of the keys to creativity.

In an analogy to physics, Arny tells us that this realm can be described in terms of *reflection*: something Flirts with you, and you Flirt back, and through that ongoing process of reflection, something new arises.[10] This murky realm of reflection lies somewhere between the worlds of mysticism, art, and psychology.

Foam and Pillows

One of the best ways I know to understand and experience this moment of reflection and murk is by working with material such as fabric, wire, socks, clay, foam, or anything else that you fancy.

Soon I will lead you through a detailed exercise using clay (or a piece of fabric, if you do not have any clay available). For the moment, however, try the following: find a pillow to experiment with or a piece of foam lying around the house (as in the picture below, left). This blank piece of foam or pillow is like the Essence, unformed, the Tao that can't be said. Begin to play with that foam or pillow, squeeze it, bend it, fold it. With an open mind, fool around with it, forming it, molding it and staying close to the experience of *not knowing* exactly what it will become.

Now notice that while doing this, small shapes or folds begin to flicker with your attention and start to look like something. The foam (or pillow) and its crevices begin to Flirt with you; simultaneously, you look at it and begin to see things in its crevices and folds. This reflection process continues until a particular fold or the shape of a particular part of the foam (or pillow) suddenly catches your attention. Something about it Flirts with you. Stay close to this Flirt, this "thing," that caught your attention.

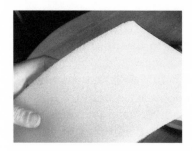 

Piece of Foam   *Small Shapes or Folds*
                                    Flicker with Your Attention

If you are not quite hooked yet, keep molding the pillow or foam and use your lucidity to notice when some small Flirt strikes your attention and just stay with it.

The next step is easy. Once you have caught the Flirt, you can midwife its birth by amplifying it—that is, bring that fold or that shape out more fully by sculpting the fabric or foam further with your hands. As you do that, you will notice some sort of creature or dreamlike image emerging. Now we are entering Dreamland. Perhaps this figure will begin to look like a sea creature or a trickster figure. Use your hands if you can to help this figure manifest more distinctly and emerge even more into the life of Consensus Reality. I remember the first foam figure that Flirted with me. It was a cloud spirit. Another day a fisherman from Marseille emerged!

Cloud Spirit   *Fisherman from Marseille*

The murky area between the Essence and the Flirt holds the as yet formless mystery that is in the midst of unfolding. If you have the courage and heart to stay in this area with a creative, empty mind, wade there, interact and reflect with it—you will discover innumerable worlds and beings wanting to come to birth. Some may surprise you!

This process reminds me of something Michelangelo said about his sculptures. He said that he did not create his sculptures. The figures were already within the blocks of stone. He simply needed to chip away the excess stone to reveal what was already within it. He is saying that each piece of raw, uncarved matter has its own life, its own seed of the Intentional Field. It is alive and full of potential. There is a similar thought in the Taoist concept of the "uncarved block," in which things in their original simplicity contain their own natural power—power that is easily spoiled and lost when that simplicity is changed.[11]

Experiment with Clay

Exercise

This exercise will give you a sense of the Intentional Field as it expresses itself through the process of reflection that arises as you mold a piece of clay. There is something mysterious and magical that happens, which is not easily verbalized, when you begin to work with the clay. Therefore, please allow me to be a bit vague in my instructions so that you can fill in the details with your own experience. You can do this exercise with your eyes open or closed. If they are open, you will notice visual Flirts. If they are closed, you will notice Flirts through the touch of your hands. Some people gain a lot from closing their eyes because it brings up new sensations and experiences that they have not experienced before.

Materials: For this experiment you will need a piece of clay, preferably about the size of your fist. If you don't have any, you can also use a piece of fabric such as a blanket. I'll describe the exercise as if you were using clay, but you can adapt the instructions to your own material. You will also need a pencil or small stick.

1. Put the clay in your hands. Mold it a bit, warm and soften it.
2. If you like, close your eyes. Relax and assume an empty, foggy mind.
3. Now, let your hands begin to smoosh, mold, and move the clay in whatever way they want to.
4. As you do that, feel/notice a flicker that catches your attention:
   a. If your eyes are closed, notice what catches your *hands'* attention. What part of the clay Flirts with your hands and wants to come out more?
   b. If you are looking at the clay, notice a Flirt that catches your attention, such as an indentation, a peak, a curve, etc.
   c. If there are a number of things that catch your hands' or your eyes' attention, wait, experiment, and discover which one wants to come out the most.
5. Once you have sensed something in the clay that wants to be born, bring it out more fully with your hands until you

create its full form. Take a couple of minutes to bring it
out fully.

6. Now look at what you have created, be with it. What is it
   that wanted to be created? Let *it* inform you about itself.
   Give it a name.
7. Put your clay creation to the side and begin to shapeshift
   into this figure; that is, become it.
   a. Begin by sitting or standing like this clay creation;
      feel like it in your body.
   b. Meditate on this experience and what it expresses to
      you. What message is it expressing?
   c. Now scratch that message in the clay with a pen or
      stick.
8. Consider the following questions:
   a. How could this figure and message be useful in your
      life and work?
   b. How does this experience relate to the first experi-
      ences you had when you woke up this morning, or
      how might it connect to a recent dream?
   c. Does this experience relate in some way to the exer-
      cise you did in Chapter 1 on movement and the
      Intentional Field?

Adding Flirts:
Parallel Worlds and Grandma Sally

You might wonder what would happen if you have many Flirts, if
many things caught your attention when you molded the clay.
Why are there so many and why are they different? And how
might all the experiences you have with the various exercises in
this book connect with one another?

We can view all of the Flirts that arise in us in one exercise or
over time as *parallel worlds*. As mentioned previously, if you add
up the various Flirts that catch your attention in one exercise or
throughout the day, even if they are very different from one
another, they add up to an important pattern or story in your life.[12]
I'll speak more about parallel worlds in Part III.

I have often started to create a puppet and waited many days
or weeks to complete it. During that time the *puppet in the midst of*

creation transformed into many different figures until it settled into its final form. Upon closer inspection, when I surveyed my puppet's various transformations, I realized that all of its parallel worlds added up to a basic pattern behind that puppet's life and myth.

For example, when I created Grandma Sally for my musical puppet theater, her first form was as a racecar driver who was going to make it in life! I waited a few days to see if this was the final puppet, but felt that I needed to go further—and the racecar driver turned into a very friendly dog.

Sally Singing "Coat of Many Colors"

The next day I was still not quite satisfied and started playing around with materials, placing a piece of fabric over the puppet's head. The puppet suddenly turned into a shy young woman with a calico scarf. As I stared at her, I "heard" her singing the song "Coat of Many Colors," about the way others made fun of her because she had poor clothing. She was hoping for love, acceptance, and warmth but was made fun of instead.

That evening my puppet transformed further into a nightclub singer with red silky clothing, feathers in her hair, and red fingernails! She loved herself and was going to slough off any critics who told her she wasn't good enough!

Nightclub Singer

The next day, while rushing by this nightclub singer puppet to get to my computer, I caught a Flirt in which I saw the puppet as a very accepting, supportive, and loving grandmother. In fact, she turned into the grandmother of one of the characters, Silly Milly, in my puppet theater. Her name was Grandma Sally.

Looking back at all of my puppet's metamorphoses, I could see that each manifestation was a part of the grandmother's myth. The grandmother represented a sense of deep love and acceptance. Each of the puppets was an aspect of this myth. One incarnation was the puppet who tried to make it in the world as a racecar driver; another felt unloved and outcast. The dog represented a loving companion, whereas the nightclub singer was going to forget all critics and become herself. Finally, the puppet blossomed into the grandmother who is all-loving and supportive.

How about your Flirts and experiences? Think about the first exercise you did, with your movement tendencies, and the previous exercise with clay. Do they connect in some way? Are they aspects of a larger story that is moving you?

The Beauty of the Mundane

Flirts happen all the time. Following them can create a way of life based on a belief in, and love of, our tiniest, flickering experiences happening in the present moment.

Sometimes the Intentional Field expresses itself in what I would call a creative or artistic manner, and sometimes its outpouring seems to follow seemingly "mundane" pathways. This variation is important to remember because we may have a tendency to value certain types of expression over others and therefore not embrace those that do not go along with our intentions or hopes.

I had a great experience of a Flirt and the Intentional Field behind it yesterday. I was feeling overworked and uneasy. It was getting late in the day, and I was tired from working all day. I felt I couldn't do anything else. Then we picked up our mail, which contained huge piles of things to do and bills to pay. I thought, "Ugh, I hate that, I'm exhausted. I don't want to get near it. Anyway, it's not creative!"

I caught a brief flickering thought that I should handle the mail now. I huffed, "Oh, no, not that! Anything but that! I won't have time to relax or even to play a bit of piano!" Then I remembered that the field of intent is like a river that flows, but it doesn't always flow in the direction that we want it to! I gathered my courage and followed that Flirt, and it turned out that the river flowed easily in the direction of answering the mail, and I actually enjoyed it. Dare I say it was even fun and energizing? It didn't feel like work; it simply happened! Flirts can give you energy in places you would never expect!

In the next chapters I offer you a number of ways to explore Flirts and the Intentional Field further with the use of various materials. It may lead you to create something artistic or playful, or it may help you answer the mail!

Notes

1. Igor Stravinsky, *Poetics of Music: In the Form of Six Lessons* (Cambridge, Massachusetts: Harvard University Press, 1970), 54-55.

2. Christ Carter, and Stephen Carter, *Creatures of Whimsy: The Art of Basil Milovsoroff (1906–1992)* (Seattle: Northwest Puppet Center, and Pixel Productions, 1998. Videocasette). Thanks to Sonja Straub for introducing me to Milovsoroff's work.

3. Michael Michalko, *Cracking Creativity: The Secrets of Creative Genius.* (Berkeley, California: Ten Speed Press, 2001), 140.

4. Keido Fukushima Roshi, conversation with author in Kyoto, Japan, 1999.

5. Shunryu Suzuki, *Zen Mind, Beginner's Mind* (New York: Weatherhill, 1970), 21.

6. Suzuki, 176.

7. Laura Clark and Suzanne Brown, *Taoism* (http://mcel.pacificu.edu/as/students/vb/Taoism.htm).

8. Paul Zollo, *Songwriters on Songwriting* (rev. ed. New York: Da Capo Press, 1997), 480.

9. Arnold Mindell, *Dreaming While Awake: Techniques for 24-Hour Lucid Dreaming* (Charlottesville, Virginia: Hampton Roads, 2000).

10. For more on reflection, see Arnold Mindell, *Dreaming While Awake,* chapter 6.

11. Benjamin Hoff, *The Tao of Pooh* (New York: Penguin, 1983).

12. For more on the way in which parallel worlds add up, see Arnold Mindell, *The Shaman's World: Paths of Creation in Psychology, Spirituality, and Physics* (forthcoming).

"I'LL DO IT LATER"
Or
"YOU COULD DO IT BETTER"

Punk Rocker

H ow many times have you said "Not now, I'll do it later"? I wish there was some way to install an alarm that would go off whenever that sentence is uttered.

Of course, it makes a lot of sense to do some things later. We can't do everything at once, and it certainly isn't always practical. But that simple phrase can be *so* hypnotic that it convinces us we truly can't do something in the moment and thereby allows us to put creative flickers off to a distant time when it could actually bloom in the moment.

Sometimes I say "I'll do it later" without noticing that I've said it! When that happens, I feel really lucky when I happen to have a friend around who hears me saying it and brings it to my attention!

The other day I was running with Arny over our lunch break before going back to work. I was thinking about puppets and suddenly a creative project flashed in my mind. I told Arny that I was tickled by the fantasy of creating a little doll that would revolve around a turntable (the old-fashioned style record player). The puppet would be dressed like an ice skater and would be attached to the turntable. She would look like she was dancing as the turntable rotated around and around. I said that I obviously didn't have the time or the materials in the moment and would have to wait and do it later.

Luckily for my sake, an alarm went off in Arny's head. He had more awareness than me in the moment and suggested that my statement "I don't have time" meant that I had *marginalized* the creative energy that wanted to emerge right then and there! He commented that assuming something must be done in the future in some other time or place can ignore the creative impulse wanting to happen in the moment.

But I had no materials, no glue, and later on I had meetings to go to! Arny simply smiled and encouraged me to let the creative idea unfold in my mind in the moment by describing the materials, the sounds, the figure that I was imagining.

I liked the idea and imagined further. I saw the little doll spinning around on the ice (turntable). In my imagination I saw her bending forward and arching backward in an elegant arabesque, all the while spinning and dancing to one of the songs I had recently composed. I imagined that the form of her body was created out of some material like wire, rubber, or latex that was wrapped in fabric and cotton. Hmm, I thought—perhaps it only takes a minute or two to unfold and bring an idea to birth, even while running in the middle of a workday!

"*You* Would Know How to Do This!"

Then came the next hurdle. I realized that I didn't know how to *technically* operate my puppet. I said to Arny, "In order to be able to move her like a puppet while she revolved around the turntable, I would need much more technical know-how than I have! That's something *you* would know how to do."

Another alarm! When you say that *someone else* would know how to do something, that could surely be the case, but check out if that *other* person isn't *a part of you* that you are marginalizing in the moment! Saying this statement might just be another way of putting things off and letting go of a creative impulse. Not unexpectedly, Arny said, "So imagine you are *me*. How would *I* operate that puppet?"

Well, I can't say that my mechanical skills are all that advanced, but I did have fun envisaging how to operate my puppet. I imagined one of the dancer's feet attached to the turntable. A puppeteer would hold her upright by holding a string attached to her head. By lowering the string, the puppet would bend at the waist. As the turntable revolved, the puppet's free leg would extend outward by itself. But how could I make one of her arms move? If I added any more strings, the turning of the table would make a huge jumbled mess! Arny did help me with this one. We imagined that one hand could have a piece of metal attached to it. The same or a second puppeteer could hold a magnet that would pull and guide that hand. I laughed and enjoyed the possibilities and elegance of this new creation.

I suddenly realized that while I was imagining her construction and running around the track, I had the subtle sense of skating on ice as well. I hadn't noticed until then that I had a subtle feeling in my limbs as if they were stretching out, almost gliding, and a light, almost floating feeling in my neck and head. When I amplified this feeling, I felt very free and easy—which was a welcome relief from the cramping and pressure I had been feeling that morning.

I never made the actual puppet, but it was even more satisfying to let the dreaming happen in the moment and to connect to the gliding feelings in my body. This helped me flow more easily through the rest of the day.

What is the moral of the story? Watch out for these statements "I'll do it later" and "You could do it better." These are key reminders to go further and let the dreaming process unfold.

Chapter 4

SOCKS

I'm gonna buy me a racing car
Gonna drive real fast
Gonna go real far
Gonna make it baby
Just wait and see!

(Harry the Hippie,
singing in my musical puppet production
as "Rolling Rex")

When I started giving classes on the Intentional Field and creativity, I had been making puppets for awhile and decided it would be fun to experiment with creating puppets together with others. I had read a few children's books about making sock puppets and decided that that was a simple and easy method for getting in touch with the creativity of the Intentional Field. Harry the Hippie was my first sock puppet.[1] In my puppet theater Harry played the role of Rolling Rex, a cool dude who is going to make it as a race car driver when he grows up!

However, I started to doubt my direction because sock puppets are so simple and the method is so well known. Then I remembered that I wanted to use the socks as a parameter or tool to experience the way in which the Intentional Field is *always* at hand, though ordinarily invisible to our everyday consciousness.

Simple Experiment

I began with a very simple experiment. I asked the class participants to put a sock on one hand. Then I asked them to simply look at the sock, to be with it, to gaze at it, and to begin to interact with it, sensing what being or creature was trying to emerge from within that sock.

Before I describe the exercise in detail, why not take a moment and try this yourself? Take off one of your socks (if you dare!) or put a spare sock over your hand. Or, if you don't have a spare sock handy, just look at the one below!

Gaze at the sock you have on your hand (or the one on the previous page) and let something about it Flirt with you—perhaps a fold in the material, a shadow, a part of the fabric will catch your attention and begin to *come alive*, will begin to *express* something. Now start to feel or sense the character that is beginning to emerge. What kind of personality does it have? Who is it that is coming to birth within that sock?

In my class the whole process occurred much faster than I had anticipated! Almost immediately people were talking in funny ways to their hands, and their sock puppets even seemed to respond. What a strange sight it was: a bunch of adults who at first looked quite reasonable and who were suddenly talking to their socks! I then asked them to turn to someone in the group and inter-act puppet to puppet. Again, this interaction happened very quickly, and there was lots of chatter and silly or extremely serious puppet conversations.

I then laid out a bunch of fabric and glue guns and said, "Now, go ahead and create that puppet figure further, using these materials in any way that you like. Use any of the materials here to bring out your puppet's nature more clearly. Add clothes, eyes, hair, or whatever." In a flash, off they went! Even those folks who felt they weren't creative at *all* immediately started to grab various materials and do stuff with them! The force of the Intentional Field moved them as it propelled and guided them down the river of their particular puppet creation.

Lee and Carole's Sock Puppets

It Creates!

Why did this happen so quickly and easily? So many of the participants had spoken previously about being blocked creatively, about
their fears that nothing would happen, that they were afraid that
they could not play, that they were not allowed to play as children,
or their fear that their creative endeavors would not be good
enough.

The short answer is that *It* creates! *We* are not doing it; instead,
we are getting out of the way so that the Intentional Field's creative
flow can emerge. Its flow was there even before we noticed it. We
simply made space for it and let it manifest through the parameter
of a sock. A helpful question to ponder is, "Where was that flow of
the Intentional Field even before we had the sock on our hands?"
We'll ask that question at the end of the following exercise.

Another key to the experience, as pointed out by the participants, is to do the process quickly. In so doing, the inner critics do
not have enough time to intervene and dump doubt on the person's experiences.

Creating a Sock Puppet
from the Intentional Field

Exercise

So let's try it. This exercise helps you get in touch with the generative and creative potential of the Intentional Field as it expresses
itself through a sock. You can do the exercise alone, with a partner,
or with a group.

Materials: You will need a sock plus some material, buttons, pipe
cleaners, feathers, tissues, or any other tidbits you find around
your home that you might use to create and decorate your puppet.
Glue, tape, a glue gun,[2] safety pins, or a needle and thread are
helpful tools for sticking stuff together. Please be careful with the
glue gun—the glue is really hot and can burn you.

To begin, plug in your glue gun (if you have one), get your
sock ready, and put all of your materials on the floor and begin:

Silly Milly

1. Take your sock and put it on your hand. Feel what it does to your hand. To make it fit better, you might fold over the material once above the knuckles and fasten it there with a safety pin.
2. Turn the puppet toward you, so that it is "looking" at you, and just be with it. Look at it. Let it Flirt with you. Perhaps something in it, like a fold or shape, will suggest a certain feeling or mood. Move your hand and notice if a particular character emerges spontaneously. Who is this on your hand? Try to catch a quick Flirt about its personality that grabs your attention. It might help to talk with it. Notice how you make faces back at it as it interacts with you. Now, if you are alone, skip to number 4.
3. Turn to someone next to you and start playing and relating, sock-creature to sock-creature, for a couple of minutes. Notice how your creature begins to unfold and take on more of a personality or begins to transform as you interact. Go with whatever emerging experience has the most energy.

4. Now, with its personality in mind, look at your sock again and imagine its features. Ask yourself:
   - Does it have one eye or two?
   - Do the eyes squint or are they wide open or closed?
   - Does your puppet have a big or little mouth?
   - What colors does it have?
   - Do things hang off of it loosely, or are the materials tightly glued to its body?
   - Does it have a cane or a hat?
   - Does it have very simple forms, or is it very complex?
5. Now turn to the materials at hand and let yourself grab whatever Flirts with you in order to bring out the puppet's character. Bring your creature out in more detail by wrapping, gluing, drawing, fastening, pasting, or tying. For example:
   - Use markers to draw on the puppet.
   - Glue buttons on for eyes and pieces of felt to create pupils.
   - Use scarves to create clothes.
   - Use shredded tissue to create hair.

Let the puppet and your relationship to it unfold and transform as you use fabric and materials to help it come into material being. A helpful metaskill is to imagine that you are a mother holding a newborn baby. This attitude may give you a sentient feeling of tenderness, of wonder, of the preciousness of the creature that is beginning to emerge. Look at it, notice its features, talk to it, and help it grow. If your puppet begins to change its form in the midst of creation, and if that feels good to you, go ahead and let it transform! As you create, see if you can feel the energy and flow that is behind what you are doing. That flow is the Intentional Field!

Oh, yes: if you are frustrated, wait a bit. Sit back and wait for *It* to guide you once again.

6. When your puppet creation is done:
   a. Bring your creature even more fully to life by doing any or all of the following:
      i. Sit across from your puppet and meditate together. Talk to it. Why is it here? Why did it

come to you today? What message does it have?
How do you feel about it? Write this down.

   ii. Let your puppet tell a story of its life. Where did
it come from? How old is it? Let it tell you about
its possible future. What will it be like a hundred
years from today?

   iii. Let your puppet move, dance, give a lecture,
write a poem, make a drawing, or sing a song!

  b. Go another step. Take the sock off your hand and put
it to the side. Now become the puppet figure yourself! Sit like it, feel like it, move like it. Experience it
from the inside out. How does this influence you?
Consider how you might use or need this experience
in your own life.

7. Now ask yourself the following questions or discuss them
with a partner:

  a. Could you feel the force of the Intentional Field moving you to create?

  b. Do you remember any of your final puppet's parallel
worlds? That is, were there other personalities or figures that arose while you were making your puppet,
before it manifested in its final form? Can you see any
relationship between these parallel worlds?

  c. Where was this puppet experience before you made
it? In other words, have you sensed this experience or
quality occurring inside you previously in your subtle body sensations, in your dreams, in the way you
tend to interact with others? Or have you noticed this
quality in other people with whom you interact?

  d. Take time to consider: In what way is this puppet
indicative of the next phase of your life?

Afterthoughts

This exercise was intended to help you get in touch with the awesome flow of the Intentional Field and to notice how this stream is
always there, ready for you to enter into at any time. You may
have discovered that the puppet experience was already there in
your body or your relationships before making the puppet, even
though you were unaware of it. You may have noticed that parallel

worlds arose before you settled on the final creation. All of these worlds add up to, and are part of, your puppet's and your own momentary dreaming path.

Arny's Moss-Head Sock Puppet

You can go really far with such puppets. When you have a chance, let them go further with dancing, singing, or writing. When I created my musical puppet theater, I waited for each puppet to sing me its song, rather than feeling I had to create the music myself. This was a very creative and freeing experience for me.

Put your puppet near your bed or desk. It can be great advisor. Talk to it often! I go back to my puppets again and again when I am confused and need help. By the way, a bottle with a thin neck is really good base to put your sock puppet on so that it can stand up by itself when you're not playing with it (see the photo above).

Becoming Your Puppet:

An Exercise to Do with a Partner

Let's go one step further. If you happen to have someone with whom you can interact, puppet to puppet, try the following exercise to take your experience a bit further and to find out more about this puppet inside yourself:

1. Put your puppet on your hand again.
2. Turn to your partner and interact puppet to puppet for a couple minutes. Let the puppets speak and move; feel the quality and energy of your puppet as you do that.

Rhea and Jennifer Interacting Puppet to Puppet

3. Now put your puppets to the side and *become the puppets yourselves.* First recall the quality of your puppet. Then sit like it and move like it and begin to talk like it. As this figure, interact for five minutes or so with your partner. Notice any hesitations you feel to being this figure as you relate to your partner, and notice if there is a feeling or figure that opposes your being this way.

   If you are shy about being the puppet, try to get to its Essence by using micromovements. That is, feel the energy of that puppet. Now put your arms to your sides, recall the puppet's energy, begin to recreate that energy with your muscles, and catch the first flickering images or feelings that emerge as you do so. This is the Essence. Then practice being that Essence with your partner.

For example, I was shy to be one of my puppets, Silly Milly. Silly Milly is happy and sings silly songs all the time. I began by acting out Silly Milly, and then I put my arms down to my sides. I then recalled her energy and, in a very slow meditation, began to recreate her energy with my arms and muscles. Just in the beginning of recreating her, I felt as though I was making a sudden spark with my hands. It felt to me like the moment when a baby is excited about something it sees—a spontaneous spark of interest that then subsides until the next spark of comes. The Essence was spontaneity, a beginner's mind that sparked whenever something exciting caught its attention. I liked the feeling of this Essence and practiced being that way with my partner.

4. Discuss together:
   a. What is the difference between being the puppeteer moving the puppet with your hand and becoming that puppet yourself? What aspect and quality did this version of the exercise bring out?
   b. How would the puppet or its Essence like to influence your way of working, interacting in relationships, and generally being in life? Consider how much of its style and energy you feel comfortable with incorporating into your life.

More Sock Fun:

Group Process Puppet Dreaming

Well, we could just stop there, but I can't help but include one more way to continue with your sock puppet. If you happen to have the luck to do all of this in a group, you might try this experiment: hold a discussion among all the puppets you created. Instead of you as people talking about issues that are on your mind, let the puppets present issues, interact with one another, and see what happens. It might be a catastrophe, but what do you really have to lose? Here goes:

1. Sit with your puppets on your hands and meditate for a couple minutes. Each of you meditates on your own puppet's feelings and what issues are important for the puppet to talk about or bring up in the group (even if the issue is about wanting to be silent).
2. Then let both your puppets discuss their issues and feelings and decide which one to focus on by noticing which one of the issues seems to have the most energy.
3. Staying true to their nature, the puppets now discuss or express themselves about that issue. Let them dance, sing, or express themselves in any way that feels right and see what happens. Maybe all the shy ones will come together? Maybe they will all start to dance.
4. When you are finished, discuss as a group:
   a. What this process might say about all of you as a group.
   b. What this process has to do with each of your own personal lives.
   c. How the puppets expressed aspects of the group that you may not have known before.
   d. How the puppets came to resolutions that you had not been aware of previously.

Puppets and Therapy

Before ending this chapter, I want to mention one of the reasons I have become especially interested in puppets these days. I have many toys, stuffed animals, and puppets that have been incredibly helpful to me in my therapy practice. Sometimes the puppets play various roles in the client's process and help to express parts that are hard to identify with. Often I use a puppet as my external supervisor whom I can ask for advice when I'm stuck. And if I sense a critic in the air, either my own or my client's, I have a trustworthy "resident critic puppet" who sits in and is never at a loss for critical things to say! In any case, I don't feel quite well as a therapist unless I feel free enough to use play and imagination; play is, of course, an important part of many therapeutic approaches.[3]

I think the roots of my interest in this area came from one of my experiences as a teenager. When I was eighteen I volunteered in the recreational unit of a children's hospital where I lived. One day two of the children who were bedridden were very angry. None of the volunteers wanted to work with these children but preferred to play with the mobile and lighthearted kids. I was in a very open mood and said that I would go and be with those kids.

The first boy I sat with was really angry because he couldn't walk. He had been in the hospital for a long time. I intuitively brought a little puppet over to him and began to talk to him through that puppet. The puppet had a very kind and understanding tone. The boy grabbed the puppet off my hand and whipped it across the room in an act of protest! I was distraught yet determined to bring some compassion to him. I picked up the puppet and tried again. Once more, the little puppet went flying through the air at top speed! *Hmm*, I thought, *this could get interesting.* I picked up the puppet again, but this time I changed my course. I whipped it across the room and it landed with a thump on the child's lap. He looked furious but giggled and whipped it back in my direction.

We continued our furious fight, finally drawing in the other bedridden child who seemed anxious to get in on the battle. A whirl of flying puppets filled the air. We all ended up laughing and enjoying ourselves and expressed some really mean things through the mouths of those flying toys. It was a wonderful experience and we became very close.

I guess it was then that I had a glimpse of the value of toys for discovering the secret dreaming process normally hidden from our awareness and of how these toys can help relieve and express some of the most difficult aspects of life.

As Jim Henson once said, "Puppets are fortunate – they can do and say things a live performer wouldn't touch with a stick."[4]

Notes

1. I was tickled to recently discover from author Alison Inches that one of Jim Henson's earliest puppets was called Harry and was a "hipster beat puppet... [who] wore dark glasses and spoke scat and jazzy nonsense syllables," in *Jim Henson's Designs and Doodles: A Muppet Sketchbook* (New York: Harry N. Abrams, Inc., 2001), 16.
2. Thanks to Annie Greenberg and Craig Huber for introducing me to glue guns!
3. See Eliana Gil, *Play in Family Therapy* (New York: Guildford Press, 1994), 45-48. She writes about the origins of puppets in child and family therapy in the United States. She also provides some very interesting case examples. Thanks to Gary Reiss for introducing me to her work.
4. Inches, 77. From a 1969 proposal for *The Muppet Show*.

SO CLOSE BUT SO FAR AWAY

On the Playground

I t is odd to me that switching dimensions can sometimes feel so easy and at other times so difficult. Noticing a Flirt can be simple and quick. All it takes to shift worlds is to notice a flickering vision or sound or movement and to let it unfold. It requires practically no energy.

Yet like the characters in the above picture, at other times stepping out of a consensual mode and into the dreaming can feel simply impossible, as if it would require a herculean heave! What a paradox!

From one viewpoint parallel worlds are really just a *breath away*. But from another viewpoint it seems as if they are on the other side of a vast and unending abyss.

What can we do? I think there is a part of all of us that knows we have many dimensions. That part is deeply democratic, fluid, and can support our fullness. It can stand back, notice, and appreciate all the facets of our experiences. It loves our consensual mind as well as the parts of us that spring easily into our dreams. It has a special feeling, a metaskill, that embraces our multidimensional natures. I am not sure how to get in touch with that part, but simply mentioning and remembering it may be a first step.

Springing Slinky

Chapter 5

IT'S ALIVE!
Discovering Life in Everyday Objects

Ruth's Sponge Puppet

T*he hills are alive with the sound of music.* Oh, how I loved to sing that song when I was a child. I realized only recently that it celebrates the inherent life force within everything. The mountains can sing; a chair can speak. Everything is alive. Why not a book or a mop?

Recently I've become interested in how "inanimate" objects and things have a life of their own, whether human-, animal-, or thing-like. I learned a lot about this from Phelim McDermott who, together with his Improbable Theater company, teaches how something as mundane as newspaper can suddenly become an amazingly alive and breathing entity.[1]

Remember Groucho Gloom whom I spoke about in the Introduction? He came to birth when my weary eyes landed on a book on my shelf as I was going to take a nap one afternoon. You might also remember Basil Milovsoroff (whom I mentioned in Chapter 3), who created the most wonderful puppets from found wood.

There are many ways to create puppets and figures from the Intentional Field. In the last chapter we began with socks. You can also start with your inner body tendencies, as we did in the first chapter, and let that experience guide you to create some kind of puppet that represents that experience. In this chapter we'll experiment with finding the life in everyday materials around our homes.

Metaskills: The Unreal Is as Real as the Real

A year or so ago I dreamed the sentence: "The unreal is as real as the real." When I woke up, I really had to twist my mind around that message to follow it! And then I got it. Everything that seems "unreal" in the eyes of Consensus Reality is *real* in some way. Now you might not believe this, but without this feeling life can get pretty dull. This way of thinking has a long history in the indigenous cultures of our world, where the natural environment—the plants, rocks, mountains, and earth—is seen as comprised of living beings. Viewing the world as sacred and mystical—as a living creation open to the unknown—opens us to the force that is dreaming us into being.

An important aspect of this experience is developing a special attention, a *second attention*,[2] in which we notice and hold dearly those things that Flirt with us, that are unusual and catch our attention. It takes a loving and compassionate feeling to stay with the things that lie outside our ordinary awareness. I do not know how to cultivate that ability, nor do I follow it all the time. My ordinary awareness holds on fiercely and blocks much of what comes fleetingly into my attention. Yet I do know that if we are able to use it, we can open up to new worlds that hold creative potential, solutions to problems, and enrich our everyday lives.

I am reminded of Stravinsky's description of a foretaste or intuition that occurs before the creative act. He seems to be speaking about the Essence and the way in which we need to hold closely to, and devoutly unfold, the Flirts that come our way:

> This foretaste of the creative act accompanies the intuitive grasp of an unknown entity already possessed but not yet intelligible, an entity that will not take definite shape except by the action of a constantly vigilant technique.[3]

Puppet Creations from Flirts at Home

Some of my best teachers about creating puppets from materials found in everyday life are the makers of the Muppets. One of my favorite books is *The Muppets Make Puppets,*[4] in which the authors describe the fun of turning just about anything you can find in your house into puppets. They are master perceivers of Flirts, whether it is a broomstick, soap dish, toothbrush, or garbage can that catches their attention. Such a freeing concept for me! Actually, I had always done this as a child. I took everything I could find and made something with it. I just had to!

Exercise

Let's start with an exercise that you can do in your home. Simply look around at all the stuff in whichever room you are in and wait for something to Flirt with you. (Choose any room; there are more than enough things in any room to keep you busy.) An important part of this exercise is accessing a cloudy, foggy mind that allows you to be in a state that is open to catching those Flirts just at the boundaries of your awareness. After trying this exercise, you may be surprised at what you *really* have in your house!

The Master of Gloom

If at any moment you feel tired and sense that you are pressing things, it may be a sign that you are not allowing the Intentional Field to guide you; instead, you are trying to make it happen. See if you can let go, relax, and once again let *It* show the way! If you seem to have such a strong critic that you are unable to let go and find a Flirt, skip the exercise and go straight to the section below called "I Can't Do It," where you will find a method of creating that makes good use of the critic's energy.

Materials: All you need for this exercise is the stuff you find around your house and, if possible, some glue or a glue gun or tape.

1. Sit quietly with your eyes closed for a couple of minutes, letting your mind become foggy and empty.
2. Then with clouded, half-opened eyes, gaze around the room and notice what Flirts with you, what quickly catches your attention. If many things catch your attention, let your unconscious mind choose which one to focus on just now.

3. Remaining in that cloudy state, continue to gaze at this thing that caught your attention. Stay with it, dream with it, sense it, and let it begin to speak to you. Imagine it has a particular mood or feeling and that it starts to come alive and talk to you. What sort of tone does it have? What kind of character is it? Stay close to it. Watch it with dimmed eyes as it expresses itself. Don't work at it; let the Intentional Field bring it to life.

    Examples: You might meet an uptight pencil, an abrupt part of a wall, a sly hat, etc. The more unusual it is, the better!

4. Imagine interacting with and talking to this being. Get to know it, its life and feelings as much as possible.

5. Now imagine how to create this thing further as a puppet or some kind of figure. If you can, begin with the actual thing that caught your attention, such as a book or a pencil. Then use any materials you want to fill it out so that it comes more to life as a puppet/figure of some sort.

    If you can't use it directly—for example, if you saw a wall but you can't use the wall—then use other materials to represent it (like a piece of cardboard or a box). Spend time creating its personality by sticking, wrapping, or tying on all sorts of things that you find around your house that spontaneously come to mind (for example, tissues, water bottles, a siphon, some fabric, a spoon); or alternatively, go outside and grab some little rocks, grass, leaves, etc. Your creation might be extremely simple, very complex, or even goofy. Don't forget that a glue gun can be a really great way to stick things on things!

    It may be that you needn't add anything to the thing that caught your attention. Perhaps it is just perfect as is!

Remember:
Experiment, play—and if it flops, so what! The fun should be in the creativity, not the end product.

---

6. Once you are satisfied with what you have created, let it express itself further in a poem or story, music, or a dance. Let this expression arise spontaneously. Or maybe

you want to choose a piece of music that you know that would go with this puppet and its mood—perhaps punk rock music! Do whatever comes naturally and spontaneously!

7. Finally—

    a. Write a couple of sentences about this process and the way in which the Intentional Field spoke to you through that object.

    b. Consider why this figure is arising in your awareness just now. What meaning might it have for your life and your creative work?

One woman, Ruth, tried this exercise at home. She made a puppet out of a sponge that she found in her house (see the picture at the beginning of this chapter). The sponge had a light and easy-going mood about it. When the sponge materialized in puppet form, it advised Ruth to relax and enjoy life and be more of a spontaneous child instead of being so serious all the time. This message was a great relief for her, because Ruth tends to take things very seriously and to work very hard. She has spent a good deal of time talking to sponge-puppet ever since!

Groucho Gloom

The first time I spontaneously experienced this exercise was when I created Groucho Gloom, whom I mentioned in the Introduction. Groucho started out as a book that caught my attention and turned into a snapping, moody version of Groucho Marx, in book form. Groucho expressed himself further in a very long poem that went on at great length. He had a lot to say and he was determined to finally say it all! I'll spare you much of the details, but here are a couple of stanzas.

Oh yes you bet I'm grouchy
Wouldn't you be?
If you were stuck on a shelf
For a year or maybe three?
Squeezed between others
Smooshed so I can't take a breath
Stuffed and mildewed
Like an early, unwanted death!

You think I'm worthless
Because I'm just a book
So you stick me here for eons,
But do you know how long it took?

To create my binding,
My pages and ink?
Not to mention the brilliant
Thoughts that I think!

What meaning could Groucho have for my life? He helped support my ability to formulate theory and think things out clearly—which I am sometimes uncertain of!

I had another very interesting experience doing this exercise with "inanimate" materials. I recently learned about stop-motion animation[5] in which you can take a series of still photos of a subject and play them back in a way that gives the impression that the material is moving by itself. Once I realized that it was possible to "animate" just about anything, my mind was overjoyed to consider ways of bringing almost anything to life—or better said, ways of *revealing the life that is already within them!*

My attention was caught by some pipe cleaners that were sitting on my table. I imagined that the pipe cleaners could dance. I began to twist and turn them, constructing three little humanlike figures, which I then wrapped with fabric. As I played with them, I started to feel their dance. I hadn't choreographed a dance in many years, and now seemed to be my opportunity!

Pipe-Cleaner Dancers

I created a background and a floor for them to stand on and positioned the dancers in this scenery. I then began to take pictures for my first stop-motion series. I started with one pose and very slightly moved the dancers into another position, moving them incrementally as I alternately clicked the camera.

The most amazing part of this experience for me, however, was that even though I *intended* to move the dancers in particular ways, the minute I began to turn and bend their bodies, I could sense their own life and movement—the movements *they* wanted to make. It felt as though their dance came alive in my hands. Once I finished the photos and converted them into a video, I added some of my music—and the result was my first stop-motion animation film. The movements of the figures came out kind of jerky, unlike the smooth motion I had hoped for, but these seemingly inanimate dancers came alive in a way that took my breath away.

Pipe-Cleaner Dancers, in Action

I Can't Do It!

What if you can't do the previous exercise? Oh, yes, for the sake of democracy, we must consider the possibility that an inner critic, like Groucho, blocks what you are doing and convinces you that objects do not have a life of their own. Such a critic might even intercept your meditation before you have a chance to notice a Flirt in your house. It might convince you that you are not creative and that it will never work. In fact, this nasty intrusion can happen at any time you think about or are in the midst of working on a creative endeavor. If this happens, chances are your mood will deteriorate quickly and you will start to feel despondent.

So—

- If you feel totally blocked...
- If nothing happens...
- If you are frustrated...
- If something is telling you that you can't do it...
- If you feel full of doubt and inner criticism at any time while reading this book...

then—turn to the exercise "Discovering the Critic's Creativity" on page 202 in Chapter 12. The steps of the exercise value the critical figure as *part of* the Intentional Field's spontaneous, creative momentary path (believe it or not!). And if you are really miserable and feel you don't have the energy to read through the steps, ask a friend to help guide you through it.

Notes

1. Phelim says that you can start with any ordinary object/substance, such as newspaper, and end up with something with a history and a story. He says that that material ceases to be a fixed entity in ordinary reality, and you discover that it has its own intention, its own way to explore the world. Personal Communication, 2004.
2. Arnold Mindell, *The Shaman's Body: A New Shamanism for Transforming Health, Relationships, and Community* (San Francisco: HarperCollins, 1993/1996), 23.
3. Igor Stravinsky, *Poetics of Music: In the Form of Six Lessons* (Cambridge, Massachusetts: Harvard University Press, 1970), 51.
4. Cheryl Henson and the Muppet Workshop, *The Muppets Make Puppets* (New York: Workman Publishing, 1994).
5. Thanks to Sara Halprin for introducing me to Stop Motion Animation.

"I DON'T KNOW THE NEXT STEP!"

Sam

Here comes another statement to watch out for: "I don't know the next step of this project."

Believe it or not, this means that you *do know* but have already marginalized that knowledge. It means you had a flickering idea or already noticed a Flirt that indicated the next step but that you *marginalized* that information! Not intentionally, though. Isn't that wild?

A question to ask yourself is, "What thing already flickered in my attention that I quickly put away? What do I recall?" Or ask yourself, "What is the next step that *I don't have*?"

If you really can't remember what previously flickered in your awareness, ask a question about the next step and look around and catch a Flirt. The world around us is generous and always has answers to our questions. Notice what catches your attention, unfold it, and it will reveal to you the next step in your journey. In other words, keep your lucid attention handy and it will show you where to go next.

Chapter 6

FLIRTING WITH THE ENVIRONMENT

The Intentional Field is all around and within us. We need only open up to it, catch the tail of its flow, and begin our creative journey. We find it in our body tendencies, we notice it in Flirts that appear in materials, and we notice it in the environment. Whether we are in the mountains or in the middle of a city street, we can discover its wisdom.

The environment has always been a sacred source of inspiration and rejuvenation for me. Sitting by a bubbling river or standing under the comfort of an old pine tree never fails to bring a kind of solace and comfort to me. I often wander in the world around me to find answers to my deepest questions, whether we are in a busy city or in the high mountains or close to the ocean.

In this chapter I'd like to enhance your experience of the environment by discovering the way in which the Intentional Field expresses itself through leaves and grass, car tires, and street corners. The environment will also bring answers to some of your questions and provide the seeds of creative projects.

Searching for Visions

In Native American cultures, an individual might go on a Vision Quest in order to gain counsel from the natural environment, to have a vision, to prepare for a significant life transition, or to get in contact with Spirit.

I frequently go out and ask the environment for guidance, answers, or creative sparks to help me with things when I am stuck. If I feel out of place or not at home somewhere, I attempt to feel the dreaming of the land in that location. This gives me the sense of being at home and helps me feel connected to the earth and its history beneath my feet.

A number of years ago I was walking along a lake in eastern Oregon and suddenly began to "hear" the moraine sing. It sang a kind of warlike chant, as if there was a battle going on. The words and melodies were about war. I went inside and wrote the music down. Later, when I read about the history of that area, I was amazed that many of the words that formed that musical piece were very similar to the words used to describe what had happened on that land years ago between the Native Americans and the U.S. Army.

When something in the environment Flirts with you, it is the land, and it is you, reflecting one another in some strange interaction that involves both. Let's call it the land-and-you-dreaming.

One way to work with the environment is to do the exercise on page 113 by going outside, noticing something that catches your attention, bringing it back to your home, and creating with it further. The following pictures show some examples:

Salome's Rock Figure

King Leaf Ghost
While running in the forest one day,
a beautiful leaf caught my attention

Flirts, Creativity, and the Environment
Exercise

In the next exercise let's go on a type of *visual* quest in the environment. If you tend to *feel* things or *hear* things, as I did, please alter the directions accordingly. Remember that anything can Flirt with you in the environment, even the most unlikely things, all the way from a beautiful branch of a tree to a piece of garbage on the street or the screeching sound of a car.[1] Everything is full of potential! It's just as useful to do this exercise in the forest as it is in the city.

This time, instead of actually bringing the thing that caught your attention back with you to your home, *remember* it and let its energy create further... and you will see how a Flirt in the environment can help you answer a question that is on your mind.[2]

Materials: In this exercise you will go outside for ten minutes. The most important materials you will need when you return are a paper and pencil or tape recorder (if you have one). You may also need miscellaneous materials such as colored paper, crayons, clay, fabric (whatever you find around the house) as well as tape, glue, or a glue gun. However, the kinds of projects you focus on may require little more than a pencil and paper.

In the following description of the exercise, I have inserted an example of my own experience in italics. Here it goes:

Inside your home:
1. Ask a question that is on your mind about a creative project, your work, or life in general and write it down.
     (*My question was: What attitude should I hold as I work on the theater project I am in the midst of creating?*)
2. Sit for a moment and access an empty, foggy mind.

Outside:
3. Now with this foggy mind, go outside and wander around for a few minutes and notice what Flirts or flickers with your attention in the environment. Notice something that quickly catches your attention. If there are many Flirts, let your unconscious mind choose the one to focus on.
     (*I saw a reddish orange flower petal that was falling to the ground.*)

4. Meditate on what it is about that thing that caught your attention. In other words, what is it that caught your attention even before you knew exactly *what* that object was in Consensus Reality? Perhaps it was the color, shape, shininess, or the movement of that object. Describe this characteristic to yourself.

   (I was struck by the gentle, tumbling motion of the flower petal as it fell to the ground. I noticed this movement before I actually knew that it was a flower petal and not a leaf.)
5. Stay with this quality/thing that caught your attention, meditate on it. Remember it; and after ten minutes go back inside.

Back inside your home:
6. Now, switching our focus to body feeling, you'll physically experience/become that thing that caught your attention.
   a. Feel your body and either notice where this Flirt experience is *already* located somewhere in your body, or begin to become it—like this: stand or sit like it, move a little bit like it, feel its energy. If it helps, put materials like a scarf or coat around you to help you feel it even more.
   b. Now let that energy begin to make a rhythm, and let that rhythm begin to move you in some way.
   c. Now we'll switch to sound. As you make that rhythm with your body, let some poetry or a song arise in conjunction with it. Give it time to develop, even if it is simple. Enjoy! Record it if you have a tape recorder or *write it down so you can remember it.*

      (I began to sway and then let my body fall loosely from side to side as if propelled by the wind. Out of my movement and rhythm came this poem:
      I'm a leaf, let me go
      Let me be taken wherever I blow
      Give up to the wind
      Be my guide
      One step and then the other
      With nothing inside)
   d. Now let this experience unfold in any way it and you would like. Use any materials that help you with this.

Take ten minutes or more. If you are confused, let *it* show the way. For example:

- Let this experience influence and add to ideas or theories you have been thinking about. Write down your new ideas.
- Let it bring new ideas for a creative project you have been working on. Write them down.
- Let it draw, dance, make a longer song or poem.
- Let it advise you about your relationship life or your work. Write down this advice.

(One of the songs in my current theater piece has to do with celebrating the seasons. I envisaged creating a headdress for the dancers that included a headband with long, thin wires attached to it. I imagined attaching artificial leaves and flowers to the ends of those wires. As the dancers moved their heads, the flowers and leaves would move in arcs and sway to the rhythm of the music. I hoped this would give the sense of the falling leaves of autumn.)

7. When you are done, look back and see how this experience answers your original question in step 1.

(If I become uncertain while working on my theater project, I can try to let go of my conscious intent and follow the direction the "wind" is blowing me, noticing any feelings, movement, or images that arise. Then I can explore how to build that new information into the larger context of my work.)

8. Finally, thank the environment for bringing you this gift.

If you would like to extend this exercise, consider what kind of clothing you would design to capture the spirit of the experience you just had.

In addition, check out the dreams you have after doing this exercise. You may be pleasantly surprised to find that this work makes it easier to understand them. After I did this exercise, I dreamed that someone who was teaching about the process of letting things happen was using real and artificial flowers!

Also remember that if you are ever in a position where you don't know the next step in a project or in your life, simply do a "Flirt quest" like this, and the answer will be right there! Answers to questions are only a breath, or a Flirt, away!

Notes

1. For a beautiful understanding and exploration of the boundless amount of sounds that we can notice in the environment around us, see composer, author, and music pioneer Pauline Oliveros' inspiring book *Deep Listening: A Composer's Sound Practice* (New York: iUniverse, 2005), 12-19, 27-56.
2. See Arny's *Dreaming While Awake* (2000c).

Chapter 7

BEHIND THE MASK

Craig's Mask

Oh, dear! I got in a really bad mood when I was writing this chapter. Every time I sat down to write, I felt depressed and upset. I didn't feel like doing it, and I couldn't figure out what the book was for. Who needs a few more exercises? For what? What do they really give the reader? Anything? I felt lazy and irritable and I didn't even want to try any of the exercises that might help! Oh god, how could I write this book for others?

I did narrowly manage to do one mask exercise, albeit a severely watered-down version of others you will find in this chapter, which turned out to be surprisingly much more potent than I had imagined. It only took a couple of minutes and didn't require that I move from my chair or use any materials at all. What a relief!

I simply put one of my hands in front of my face, as if it were a mask, and asked myself, "What experience is trying to emerge from behind my hand? What feeling or figure is behind this mask?" Simple, huh? Lo and behold, out came something I wasn't expecting, something quite different from my ordinary demeanor!

Lily's Mask

With my hand in front of my face, I began to feel my shoulders rising up, my face starting to scrunch in a menacing sort of way, and I started to feel like a big, hairy animal that was in a rage! I simultaneously heard a gravelly voice in my head shouting in a harsh, panting, angry sort of way as follows:

Let me live, set me free
From these chains that bind me!
I hate this manuscript; I hate it all,
I'm going to tear it up, get rid of it once and for all.
I am the figure behind the mask.

It's so easy, with a hand in front of your face,
To find out who's waiting, to take your place!
Out of that mystery comes an oozing, moving form
A buried being you can bring to life and adorn!
It's me behind the mask!

I want to write this book, I'll call the shots
I'm the great director, ignore me and I'll get real hot
Don't forget our dear friends Jekyll and Hyde,
The Phantom of the Opera, and hundreds of others by my side,
I am the figure you're waiting for, behind the mask!

Whoa! Where did that come from? I was pretty upset and had a few things of my own to say to that creature! Let me fill you in on our dialogue:

Me: Hey, wait a minute! Where did you come from? Your words sound pretty gory. Some people might get scared of their inner experiences if you talk like that! Maybe some nice figures want to come out, or some heavenly creatures? What is all this nasty stuff about?

Monster: I am sick of nice things!!! I feel so confined by them. Let me out, let me free! So what if people get scared? This is what life is about! This energy! Every time you say that, I can't breathe!

Me: No, this is not what life is about. People have enough pain in their lives!

Monster: Yeah, but they never let me express myself. That's why I get so enraged. Just think of the creativity and energy I could bring if only you'd let me out! I'm like a tornado just waiting to do something interesting!

Me: That's a good point.

Monster: Yes a very good point! And anyway, you never know what will come next. It's all about process, remember? You know the process theory that says that things that look static are just states in the midst of unfolding. I am one of those states! I'm not such a bad guy. I have a lot of pent-up energy because you don't let me let it out! But if you give me a chance to unfold, I could use it in a really exciting and creative way. Other people will probably have very different experiences, and they could be real interesting, too. Just look at the picture of the mask at the beginning of this chapter. Doesn't look like such a bad character, does it? Pretty interesting, I would say. So let us express ourselves for once, okay?

Me: Yeah. You remind me that we ordinary humans carry with us two masks. One is our ordinary identity that we don't even know we're wearing most of the time. Then there are other masks, hidden behind that ordinary identity, that want to come out as well but that we usually just bury and ignore.[1] I'm ready to find out about both of them.

Monster: Great! The more dreaming, the better for my friends and me!

It's deceivingly simple. Just take a moment to put your hand up in front of your face and notice the subtle tendencies and feelings that begin to move you behind that hand. Off you go into another parallel world that was always there, but that you hadn't noticed before.[2] Why not try it for a moment? What being is waiting to come alive behind your hand?

Masks are amazing. When you put on a mask, there is a subtle interaction. You begin to feel something moving you, the Intentional Field, as the mask Flirts with you and you Flirt with it. And then something magical and unexpected is born! Theater director Peter Brook says, "A mask is two-way traffic all the time; it sends a message in and projects a message out."[3]

Masks are bridges between our known world and the world of myth and dreams.[4] They are a crosscultural medium that has been used all over the world for this purpose in rituals, ceremonies, theater, initiation rites, to contact spirits and animals, to entertain, for theater, and to bring the dreaming into everyday life. Let's try

Natasha's Mask

using them to get in touch with the Intentional Field and the beings who are waiting to come into life.

Dream Mask Exercise: Part 1

In the following exercises, I suggest two very simple methods for making masks.[5] I think the simplest methods are often the most powerful. Such uncomplicated techniques can be used as express trains to our dreaming processes. In the following experiment, which builds on other exercises done previously, we will again venture into that murky realm between the Essence and Flirts.

As I have noted previously, it is difficult to describe the steps of the exercise because the exact progression will emerge from your inner experiences. Let your own process be your guide and use my words to find your own dreaming process.

Materials: For this exercise, you will need a paper plate, some elastic thread or string, and a hole-puncher or a pointed scissors.
  1. Hold your paper plate up to your face and locate where to put eyes. Now put the plate down and punch or cut holes with your scissors in the location where the eyes will be.

Just below the eyes, and one inch from the sides of the mask, make a hole on each side with a hole-punch or the pointed end of a scissors and tie on elastic thread or string. You will tie this around the back of your head. Or forget the string and simply hold the plate up to your face.

2. When you are ready, put your plate in front of your face and just be with it. Assume a slightly empty, foggy state of mind and notice what happens to you when you are holding the plate in front of you. What do you feel? Notice slight tendencies in your body to move. Notice how the mask begins to affect and Flirt with you.

3. Stay close to these tendencies and Flirts and feelings, and begin to let these move through your body. Feel the force that is moving you as you begin to fill out this experience behind the mask with movement and feeling. Stay with your experience even if it seems irrational. Notice how it affects your breathing.

4. Continue to unfold your movements and feelings, and now make an *image* of this experience (if you have not already) of some kind of figure or thing that you are expressing.

   a. Begin to shapeshift into this creature. That is, feel as deeply into that figure as you can, and use your whole body to *become* it. See through *its* eyes and let it make sounds and/or speak through you. If the creature is very surprising or unusual, trust that it will show its direction and wisdom if you allow it to unfold.

   b. Let it unfold further by singing a song or giving a speech or just moving around. Try to find out its central message. Why has it appeared today?

   c. Make a note about its message and consider that this may be the answer to a question you have had about yourself.

5. If you are doing this exercise with others, share your experiences with one another.

Dream Mask Exercise: Part 2

Let's go one step further with the above exercise by decorating our masks with actual materials. The mask may turn out to be very simple or elaborate, realistic or abstract. Let the energy of that figure create the mask, and it will guide you as to what the final product will be!

Materials: You will need your paper plate and a bunch of materials such as paper, scissors, yarn, fabric, tissue paper, crayons, paint or markers, glue, etc.

1. Meditate for a few minutes, recalling the feeling that came out of your paper-plate experience. Remember the sounds or words of that figure, what it said or did, its energy, its movements, etc. Put your plate up to your face again and feel that experience for a moment.

Liz's Mask

2. When you are ready, put the paper plate down and let yourself be drawn to certain materials that Flirt with you and that you would like to use for creating your mask. Notice which materials catch fire and start to construct your mask. Continue creating and embellishing on it for about fifteen minutes.
3. When you are done, put your mask on and become it. Feel what it is like to be this figure. Let it influence your movement and sound. Let it create a short poem and write that poem down.
4. When you are done, ask yourself the following questions or discuss them with a partner:

a. As you went through this process, could you feel the Intentional Field moving you, propelling you to create that mask?

b. What was it that was trying to come into being? Why did it arise today?

c. Where was this experience inside you before you made the mask? (For example, in your relationships, body symptoms, dreams.)

When I did this exercise the other day, I put the plate up to my face and felt my head go backward and imagined myself turning upside down. I felt like a little girl who was standing on her head, seeing the world from upside-down. This really changed my perception and feeling about things! I felt I was closer to the plant world and that everything in the ordinary right-side-up world seemed much more serious and linear than it needed to be. I made a very big mask. In fact when I looked through its upside-down eyes, the mask extended upward about four feet over my head! I wore this mask and wrote the following poem:

Seeing the world from upside down
The top of my head, stuck in the ground
Toes reaching upward, toward the sky
Watching from below as the world passes by
It's another place when you're upside down
Everything looks crazy, the other way 'round
Now the blood rushes to my mind
And that's what it's like, to step out of time.

Everyday Mask and Dream Mask Interaction

We all wear masks every day. In Process Work we call our every-day mask our primary process, our ordinary identity. Most often we don't realize we have it on! Our primary process is not totally conscious. It happens to us and becomes an automatic long-term pattern—but it is certainly not the whole of us.

Frequently, our primary process is not connected with our deeper dreaming experiences. That's why we often feel out of sync

Upside-Down Mask

with ourselves. Our identity and our dreaming processes are parallel worlds that rarely meet or interact.

Let's try to have them interact and come a bit closer together. In the following exercise we'll create an everyday mask and let it interact with the dream mask that we created in the previous exercise. We'll try to find a bridge between these two very different realities.

Exercise

This exercise is easiest done with a partner, but you can adapt the instructions to working with yourself alone by following the italicized instructions in parentheses.

Materials: You'll need your dream mask, a second paper plate, and a sharp pointed scissors.

1. Hold your dream mask up to your face once again. Meditate on its qualities; recall its feeling, sounds, words, gestures, etc. Then put it down.
2. Now take another paper plate, poke two eyes in it, put it in front of your face, and imagine that it represents your

everyday, ordinary personality. Make a few hand gestures that mirror that part of you, and move the mask in
conjunction with those gestures. This may give you the
sense that your everyday identity is also a mask that you
wear all the time but are normally unconscious of.

Dai's Mask

3. Now hold both masks in each of your hands. Alternately
   put one up to your face and feel its quality, and then do
   the same thing with the other.
4. Show your partner your everyday mask and gestures so
   that she or he can act that part out for you. Give your partner that paper plate and tell her or him where to stand to
   act out this everyday part of you.
   (If you are alone, place the everyday mask in one hand.)
5. Put on your dream mask and stand in a particular spot in
   relationship to your partner; the spot you choose should
   feel like the right place to stand for that dream mask.
   (Put the dream mask in your other hand.)
6. Both of you meditate behind the masks for a moment and
   then begin to move sentiently—that is, in slow motion,
   following the tendencies you feel behind the mask, and in
   relationship to one another for a couple of minutes. The
   Intentional Field and your subtle and sentient feelings
   will guide you.

(Begin to move the masks slowly and sentiently in rela-
tionship to one another.)

7. After a few minutes start to speak to one another as these
    masks, in relationship to one another. At any time you can
    exchange masks and switch roles. Discover what the
    dream mask might want to bring to everyday life, and
    vice versa. Take time to negotiate the relationship
    between these two figures if there is conflict. Continue the
    interaction until you discover something new.

    (Speak for both masks and let them interact.)

8. Finally, talk to your partner about the meaning of this
    experience for your life as a whole and your work.

    *(Think about the meaning of this experience for your life
    and work.)*

A Laundry Pause

Nothing happens linearly! Just as I finished the above section of
this work and wanted to continue with an exercise involving paper
bags, I went downstairs to get the laundry out of the dryer. As I
was going out the door, I went over to look once again at a puppet
that I am in the midst of creating but have not quite finished. I just
have not been able to find its character, the right clothes to put on
it, or even a head! Poor puppet has been sitting there headless for
the last week or two, as I tried many variations of outfits and
heads, none of which really clicked. And so it has been lying there
for a week or so in a half-made, headless state!

As I continued toward the dryer, my eyes fleetingly glimpsed
a corrugated cardboard box that I had broken down and put into
the recycle bin. It was the box that had contained a beautiful bowl
with colorful chili peppers painted on it that I had purchased the
day before. I quickly glanced at the box, which had a picture of this
beautiful bowl on it. Then I looked again and giggled because the
colors and images of the chilis made me feel really happy. As I was
pulling the sheets out of the dryer, I realized that my seemingly
innocent glances at that box were Flirts! Oh, how much consciousness it takes to catch such fleeting things!

It suddenly dawned on me, "How about making the clothes
and the head out of this colorful box? If I liked it so much, why not
create the rest of the puppet out of it? And how about making a

puppet that was all about fruits and vegetables?" Many thoughts raced through my mind. Something had caught fire. How about that cooking magazine that just arrived yesterday? Maybe I could glue pictures from it onto material and create its clothes!

I quickly pulled out some material from my storage bins, found my magazine, cut out pictures of fruit, herb, and vegetable pictures, and began to paste them onto the material. I had to wait for the glue to dry before going on to the next step, so I proceeded to fold the laundry—and now I am once more upstairs working on this chapter! What an unpredictable life this is!

Paper Bag Mask Exercise

Okay, let's get back to mask making. In this exercise we'll create a simple mask with a paper bag and explore the Intentional Field within that mask.

By the way, when I made a paper bag mask, I had a little trouble keeping the bag steady on my head. Every time I tried to move with it, it shifted so much that I couldn't see out of the eyeholes. Although this could be an interesting experience too, I wanted a steady paper bag that wouldn't shift much when I moved, so I developed a method of my pulling hair through the top of the bag and fastening it with a ponytail holder to hold the bag in place. I must say, this alone creates a pretty funny mask all by itself!

Oh, dear, what should you do if you are "hair-challenged" (that is, balding or short haired!)? One of the methods I learned from a mask-making book is to make a headband out of sturdy paper, which you can then staple to the inside of the bag to hold it in place, and which will, in turn, help to hold the bag on your head. Phew!

Materials: You will need a paper bag, scissors, a ponytail holder if you have hair, or some sturdy paper, tape, and a stapler to make a headband if you don't have hair. To decorate the bag, you will need any materials that you can think of, from yarn to fabric to feathers, paints to crayons, or whatever catches your attention.

1. Put the bag on your head, and then take it off and cut the bag down to size so that it extends either to the bottom of your chin or to just above your shoulders.
2. Cut out holes for the eyes. You can cut creative shapes or simply cut out a couple of ordinary holes. Now put a hole

Amy H.'s Paper-Bag Mask

in the top of the bag in which you will thread some of your hair. If you have short or no hair, make a round headband out of sturdy paper: measure around your head, cut two strips of paper that you can glue together into one long piece and wrap around into a circle, and then staple that headband to the inside of the bag.

3. Sit on the floor. Put the bag on your head. If you have longer hair and a hole on the top of your bag, thread some of your hair through the hole and fasten the hair with a ponytail holder to hold it tightly.

4. Now simply sit with that mask on and begin to let the mask communicate with you, Flirt with you. Notice your subtle movement tendencies as you interact with it, and let these movements begin to unfold throughout your body. You can move on the floor or stand and move.

5. Continue to move until you have an image of what these movement tendencies are about. Perhaps you will discover some sort of creature or being that you are becoming. Become that image or thing and let it make sounds.

Kanae Moving with Her Mask

6. Now unfold it further by imagining you are in the middle of a very short story about that figure/experience. Act this out as you move and tell the story to yourself. (If you want, you can put on some music and continue to unfold your experience.)

   Note: If you feel claustrophobic at any time with the mask on, you can always take it off and continue that same experience with the mask off. The mask will simply give you an impulse that you can continue to unfold, even without the actual mask on your head.

7. When you have a good sense of the experience that was trying to manifest from that mask, take it off and use your materials to decorate and embellish it in order to bring its characteristics out even more. When you are done, put it on again and get to know yourself even more as this being.

8. Finally, take the bag off once again and meditate on what this experience might mean for you today. Share it with someone else if you are doing this exercise with others.

Christine's Mask

Notes

1. Theater producer and director Peter Brook also says that the plain white mask or piece of paper is a most wonderful exercise for actors: "Just put a bit of white paper on his face and say, 'Now look around.' He can't fail to be instantly aware of everything he normally forgets." In "Lie and Glorious Adjective: An Interview with Peter Brook: The Transformative Power of Mask," *Parabola* (Summer 1981): 62.
2. Arny mentioned that you can also go behind a curtain and ask yourself what kinds of experiences you have when you are behind it and if they differ from your regular, in-front-of-the-curtain experiences. This method works particularly well with children.
3. Lorna Marshall and David Williams, "Peter Brook: Transparency and the Invisible Network," in *Twentieth Century Actor Training* (edited by Alison Hodge, New York: Routledge, 2000), 187–188.
4. Masks in Bali are "the interface between the timeless world of myth and the immediate world of fact," writes Ron Jenkins in "Two Way Mirrors," *Parabola* (August, 1981): 18.
5. Thanks to Rhea for experimenting with and developing some of these exercises with me for our creativity class in spring 2003 at the Process Work Center of Portland and for introducing me to some of the literature about acting and mask making.

Interlude

STOP OR GO?

Horatio the Shadow Puppet

There is no recipe for everyone when it comes to creative impasses. Sometimes we need to push on. Other times we need to wait. Each person has her or his own unique experience of the Intentional Field and her or his own process and timing.

At times I need to go the extra mile. I've noticed that I often want to give up when I get to an impasse, when I don't know how to continue. I can become extremely frustrated and impatient! One of the best methods that has helped me is to stay *just a little longer*. If I can just hang in there a bit longer, I often find another direction of the stream that I had not seen before.

For example, I remember a scarf puppet that I made one day. After I created her, the whole project fell flat. By waiting just a bit longer than I ordinarily would, and playing with her movement, I began to imagine her reaching upward toward the sky and started to hear her sing something about reaching for the stars. Just two minutes earlier I had almost walked away from the project completely. Perhaps we need inner support from ourselves and from one another to go this extra mile.

However, if you try three times and you just can't seem to get the motor of a project going again, it may be important to sit back, wait, and let things ripen and mature by themselves. Perhaps you need to go to sleep and dream the next step. Maybe something totally unrelated that you do that day will give you just the key you were looking for. Perhaps you have to allow something else to unfold before you are able to complete what you are doing.

I heard a great story about Thomas Edison. When he wanted to discover a new idea, he would take a nap. Actually, first he would place a metal ball in each of his hands and a metal plate just underneath his hands on the floor. Then he would take a nap. Just as he started to fall asleep, the metal balls would fall to the ground and awaken him. Then he would catch the thoughts that were going through his mind just as he was falling asleep and that would be the new inspiration for his work![1]

Everything has its own timing. A friend of mine told me that the poet Rainer Maria Rilke did not wait one night or even a week, but ten *years* to write some of his sonnets and elegies![2]

Of course, sometimes we just have to do something in a rush, and that's great. But waiting can be invaluable, too.

Notes

1. Twyla Tharp, *The Creative Habit: Learn It and Use It for Life* (New York: Simon & Schuster, 2003), 101.
2. Thanks to David Clark for telling me about this.

Chapter 8

THE FLYING UMBRELLA STORY

Silly Milly and her "Flying Umbrella"

For one of our recent seminars on "Big Medicine," Arny and I developed exercises to experience the wisdom and force of the Intentional Field. One evening during our preparations, I told him about a book on creativity I was reading—in particular, an exercise in that book that focused on the spontaneous connections that arise between chance objects and random words. Michael Michalko describes the process of using random words to tell a story.[1]

Arny and I decided to embellish that concept in order to experience how the Intentional Field spontaneously weaves words together into a story or fairy tale. You may remember the analogy of the Intentional Field in terms of the way in which magnetic filings invisibly organize themselves when a magnet is based beneath them. The configuration of those filings is similar to this spontaneously arising word story.

Actually, this process happens each night when we go to sleep. During the night our dreaming magically weaves impressions and feelings we had during the day into a dream tale.

Revisiting Intentional Fields and Parameters

Let's revisit the idea of the Intentional Field and its parameters in a given moment. We have spoken a little about the way in which the Intentional Field reveals itself through various parameters, and we have experimented with various media such as socks, the environment, paper plates, paper bags, and such.

I am reminded of something Igor Stravinsky wrote about the absolute necessity of parameters in the creative process. He speaks of unbearable and overwhelming feelings that can occur if we do not have parameters at hand through which to express ourselves:

> As for myself, I experience a sort of terror when, at the moment of setting to work and finding myself before the infinitude of possibilities that present themselves, I have the feeling that everything is permissible to me.... If nothing offers me any resistance, then any effort is inconceivable, and I cannot use anything as a basis, and consequently every undertaking becomes futile.
>
> Will I then have to lose myself in the abyss of freedom? To what shall I cling in order to escape the dizziness that seizes me before the virtuality of this infinitude?[2]

The parameters Stravinsky used were the twelve notes of the scale, which provided the form through which his music could express itself:

> However, I shall not succumb. I shall overcome my terror and shall be reassured by the thought that I have the seven notes of the scale and its chromatic intervals at my disposal, that strong and weak accents are within my reach, and that in all of these I possess solid and concrete elements which offer me a field of experience just as vast as the upsetting and dizzy infinitude that had just frightened me. It is into this field that I shall sink my roots, fully convinced that combinations which have at their disposal twelve sounds in each octave and all possible rhythmic varieties promise me riches that all the activity of human genius will never exhaust.[3]

The use of parameters and the spontaneous organization of those parameters are keys for many artists in generating and discovering new and creative pathways. Composer John Cage and choreographer Merce Cunningham, partners and collaborators, have employed chance techniques such as a coin toss and the I Ching (the Chinese divination procedure) to develop their music and dance sequences.[4]

Actors and directors Phelim McDermott and Julian Crouch speak about placing random items on stage before a performance without having any idea what they would do with them until the actual performance. The Intentional Field will begin to work with these objects in some unexpected way. This unexpectedness is the very basis of all improvisational theater and dance—art forms that rely on the playful metaskills of the performers:

> For example, decide that there will be a number of trap doors or a large piece of silk without yet knowing how you are going to use them in the show. This involves trusting that the creative process will reveal to you or will tell you why you made these intuitive decisions. It also requires the honesty to tell a company that you don't know why you did certain things but you hope to find out with their help. The way to find these things out is through play.[5]

Any really good improvisational performance relies on the spontaneous formation of individual elements.

The Flying Umbrella

Let's turn to our exercise. Let me tell you the way in which the name of this exercise, "The Flying Umbrella," came about. After we developed the steps of the exercise, I dreamed that someone gave Arny a big black umbrella. When Arny held the umbrella up, it lifted him off the ground and took him flying in the air! We realized then that the exercise had the potential to help all of us levitate to other dimensions, and so we called it the Flying Umbrella!

In this exercise you will set up a parameter of five words and notice how the Intentional Field weaves the words together into a spontaneous story. You will notice the way in which the story just happens effortlessly without much thought. You can do this exercise alone, or, it is also a lot of fun and interesting to do with a group. I include that group exercise as well, below, in case you want to try it with a few friends.

Arny and I discovered that this exercise can be a helpful way to work on yourself at almost any time, even if you are feeling miserable and nothing seems to help, if you are in a bad complex, if you feel depressed, blocked, or at a creative impasse. It will provide insight into your difficulties and potential solutions.

By the way, you can do this exercise very quickly, which can have advantages when you don't really have much time or energy to work on yourself!

A crucial step in this exercise is to access an empty mind, which will help you drop your organized mind for a moment and allow the Intentional Field to creatively weave a story. The story will most likely bring solutions and ideas that you would have never thought of with your conscious mind.

Many musicians, artists, scientists, and inventors who cannot solve a problem or are at a creative impasse speak about letting go in order to allow the next steps to manifest; sometimes relaxing and having a sudden insight, sometimes going to sleep and having a dream. For example,

> Archimedes got his sudden insight about the principle of displacement while daydreaming in his bath... Henri Poincare, a French genius, spoke of incredible ideas and insights that came to him with suddenness and immediate certainty out of the blue.... Other geniuses offer similar experiences. Like a sudden

flash of lightning, ideas and solutions seemingly appear out of nowhere.[6]

Likewise we will collect individual elements (words), let go of our conscious intentions, and notice how resolutions appear easily by letting the wisdom of the Intentional Field present itself.

Exercise

This exercise is written as if you were doing it with the help of a partner. However, you can adapt the instructions to working on yourself alone. At one point you will begin to weave a story. Take only a few minutes to create the story so as to ensure that the Intentional Field spontaneously creates without your ordinary mind getting in the way. The story might be irrational or fairytale-like. That's just fine! Trust it. Let it evolve and find its own unique nature, and it will reveal all sorts of insights. (See Chapter 10 for another version of this exercise [using sound instead of words].)

Materials: You will need a paper and pen.
1. Both people sit and meditate for three minutes (or meditate alone) accessing an empty, foggy mind.
2. One person, the storyteller, poses a question—mundane or profound—that she or he would like answered in the next weeks.
3. That person names two important words about that problem and writes them down on a piece of paper.
4. Then the partner assumes a cloudy mind, gazes around the room and notices a Flirt that catches her or his attention. (If you are alone, do this yourself.) The partner should do this three times and write one-word descriptions for each of those Flirts on the same paper in a haphazard order (for instance *triangle, coffee, bottle,* etc.).
5. The original person (the storyteller) should now look at the five words on the paper. The partner should encourage the storyteller, saying: "Dear friend, please tell me a story using these five words."
   a. The storyteller should look at the words with a cloudy mind, make a sound like "Ahhhh," and let a story unfold spontaneously, *in a few minutes,* using all

        five words. The partner should listen to, repeat, and show interest in the story.

    b. Once complete, the storyteller should *retell* the story with enjoyment, acting it out with movement and drama! Enjoy the creativity of it all!

    c. If the storyteller still has questions or is confused at the end of the story, she or he should begin to tell the story again, this time weaving in a figure that has this same question, and continue to creatively unfold the story until the question is answered to her or his satisfaction.

6. Finally, the storyteller should ask herself or himself how this story might—

    a. Be a symbolic solution to the problem she or he mentioned in the beginning.

    b. Be a metaphor for what is trying to happen in her or his life as a whole.

7. Make notes about what you learned.

Group Flying Umbrella Exercise

For a long time I wanted to try the Flying Umbrella exercise with a whole group. I wondered what would happen if a group came up with a collective question and wove the story together as a unit. Perhaps the field would bring an answer for each of us as individuals as well as for the group as a whole.

My friend Rhea and I experimented with this in one of our classes. We all sat in a semicircle. Since we had just done the paper-bag exercise, we did the group Flying Umbrella exercise with our paper-bag masks on (this added element is definitely not a requirement). We looked pretty strange!

We agreed upon a question that was meaningful to us and wrote down two important words from that question. Then various people in the group came up with the Flirt words. We wrote all the words down on big signs and held them in the air so that everyone could see them. All of us, then, went into a foggy state and let a story express itself through us as each person felt called to begin, add, or finish the story, adding on sentence after sentence and Flirt word after Flirt word. It was a lot of fun, surprising, and gave us unexpected insights into our question.

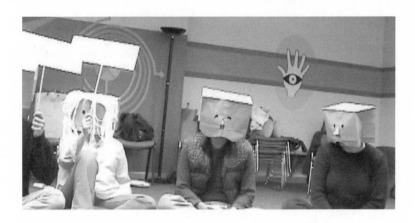

Group Flying Umbrella Exercise

Once again, don't take much time to weave the story; it should come spontaneously. You can do this in pairs or larger groups.

Materials: You will need five big pieces of paper and a pen or marker. Put these papers and pen in the middle of the group.

1. Everyone in your group should take time to access a cloudy mind. While in this foggy state, each should meditate for a couple of minutes on a question about the group that she or he would like to ask, such as—
   - What is meant for us as a group?
   - How should we get to know one another?
   - What does the Tao want us to know just now?
   - What task should we be focusing on?
2. Discuss the questions together and after five minutes choose one of these on which to focus. If you are unable to decide on one question, spin the pen and see to whom it points. The question asked by that person is the one to choose.
3. Decide as a group on two central words from that question/problem. Someone should then write these words down on big pieces of paper and put them in the middle of the group.

4. Spin the pen. The person to whom the pen points should take a moment to access a foggy and unfocused mind, look around, and notice a visual Flirt that catches his or her attention. Give this Flirt a one-word name. Tell the name to the group and someone write this word on one of the big pieces of paper. Do this step two more times for a total of five words.

5. People in the group should now hold up the big papers with the words written on them. Everyone should once again assume a cloudy mind, gaze at the words on the big papers, and begin to weave a story with the five words. Here's how:

   a. When one person feels moved to speak, she or he should begin to tell the story, saying one or two sentences that incorporate one of the Flirt words. You might begin, "Once upon a time..."

   b. Another person who feels moved to fill out the story adds a couple of sentences that includes another Flirt word. Remember to stay in a cloudy mind when you are doing this!

   c. Others continue to weave the story as they feel moved to join. It's okay to repeat Flirt words during this process. The story will complete itself when it finds a natural conclusion, or within a maximum of six minutes.

6. As a group recall and repeat the story, this time acting it out together with movement and sound.

7. Finally, discuss—

   a. How this story symbolically answers the group's original question.

   b. How the story applies in some way to each person's personal life and work.

   c. If there are still questions that the group doesn't understand, go back into the story, weave the question into it, and continue to unfold the story until you come to a satisfying conclusion.

Notes

1. Michael Michalko, *Cracking Creativity: The Secrets of Creative Genius* (Berkeley, California: Ten Speed Press, 2001), 139–172.
2. Igor Stravinsky, *Poetics of Music: In the Form of Six Lessons* (Cambridge, Massachusetts: Harvard University Press, 1970), 63-64.
3. Stravinsky, 64.
4. For example, John Cage "would assign musical value (pitch and duration) to all possible combinations of the three coins and write the music much as if he were taking dictation." Jeffery Byrd, "Cage, John," *glbtq.com* ("an encyclopedia of gay, lesbian, bisexual, transgender, & queer culture," http://www.glbtq.com/arts/cage_j.html). Merce Cunningham said: "There are one through 64 possibilities. So often in dances I made 64 separate phrases, which I put down or tried to put in the computer, each of which is separate— one doesn't follow any other. Then, you take that as a body of material and cast your fortune as to which comes up." Cynthia Joyce, "I like to Make Steps," interview with Merce Cunningham, *Salon.com* (http://www.salon.com/weekly/interview960722.html).
5. Phelim McDermott and Julian Crouch, "Puppetry: A User's Guide" (http://www.improbable.co.uk/article.asp?article_id=3).
6. Michalko, 109.

Part III

PARALLEL WORLDS AND CREATIVITY

Chapter 9

STEPPING INTO THE LIFE OF SOMEONE ELSE

One day I'll write a concerto
To make your hearts soar
And all I ask of you, my friends,
Is to listen,
Nothing more
When will the day come
When all my thoughts will turn into music?
(My puppet The Musician singing the song
"When My Thoughts Turn into Music")

How relieving it can be to drop our identities for a moment and become someone or something else. How about a deep-sea diver, a philosopher, or a painter on the Champs Elysee? There are so many worlds inside of us, yet we most often choose to focus on only one of them. These parallel worlds lie waiting just a breath away if we have the courage to pause and open up to them. The concept of parallel worlds is one of my favorites, probably because it has helped me more than anything else to understand much of my own creative process and the endless generosity of the Intentional Field.

The notion of parallel worlds emerged from a paradox found in quantum physics, in which the quantum wave function can appear both as wave *and* particle. Hugh Everett and Bryce Dewitt interpreted this phenomenon, theorizing that the reason the wave function can appear in two different states is because both states exist simultaneously as parallel worlds.

They explained that we tend to focus on the most *probable* world while marginalizing the existence of the others. That does not mean that the other worlds do not exist, but simply that we are not focusing on them. When I focus on *A*, I do not notice *B*. In fact, there are an infinite number of parallel worlds occurring simultaneously. They called their theory the Many Worlds Theory.[1]

If we apply this theory to the exercises in this book, we can see that just about every exercise has, at its core, the experience of stepping into a parallel world that we did not realize existed prior to that moment. When we played with clay, a figure emerged that embodied another worldview and landscape. When we put a paper plate up to our faces, we sensed another being with an entire world of its own, trying to emerge.

Recall for a moment the three dimensions of experience that I spoke about in Chapter 1: Consensus Reality, Dreamland, and the Essence. All of these dimensions are parallel to one another. They exist simultaneously, yet we typically focus on only one and marginalize the others. Parallel worlds also exist within any *one* dimension. For example, in Dreamland we find an assortment of figures from our dreams, all parallel to one another.

A sense of wellness and freedom comes from having access to and fluidity with our parallel worlds. By stepping into them, we let go of our identities for a moment and discover a new world full of potential and a great deal of creativity. Parallel worlds remind us of how multidimensional we really are, and of the vastness of our creative potential. Arny calls the metaskill of openness to our various parts and dimensions, *deep democracy.*[2]

Three-Headed Team

Parallel worlds can also come in handy if you find yourself stuck with a given problem. In order to solve a problem in one dimension, such as Consensus Reality, try going to another dimension—to a *hyperspace*, to find new resolutions![3]

In this chapter I would like to focus on one particular method of stepping into a parallel world that has been particularly useful for me in my creative endeavors.[4]

Three Dimensions and Cubism

The beauty of a multidimensional experience of life is expressed most elegantly in the ideas and techniques of Cubism, an artistic form in which many dimensions or perspectives of a given subject are portrayed simultaneously. The Cubists believed that you could not truly understand a subject unless you viewed it from many sides all at once. The artist Cezanne "brought forth a new consciousness of the multiplicity of perspectives inherent in viewing the world."[5]

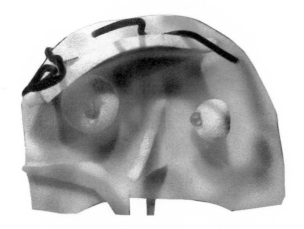

My Cubist Head

Cezanne's genius was to recognize the creative possibilities these differences of perception offered the artist in viewing the world, and he changed the nature of art.[6]

Cubism developed in the early 1900s when visual artists such as Picasso, Braque, and Chagall were breaking out of the consensual, static view of reality. They stated that only when multiple perspectives of any given subject were shown did the "true" nature of their subject reveal itself. One view was not enough. The ideas of Cubism have influenced many areas of the arts, including music and writing.[7] It is also remarkable to note that at the same time that Cubism developed, Albert Einstein was discovering the theory of relativity—now fundamental to our understanding of the universe—in which everything must be understood in terms of its relationship to everything else. Centuries prior to Cubism, Leonardo Da Vinci said that we can only understand something if we perceive it from a minimum of three perspectives. Otherwise we are unconscious of its entirety.[8]

Process Work, Parallel Worlds,
and Altered States

Actually, we are all walking parallel worlds! In any given moment we have a primary process or identity and a secondary process that appears in the form of double or unintended signals. If we are aware of one (say, a cordial smile on our face), we are most often not simultaneously aware of the other (say, the way our eyes are looking down, indicating a desire to be internal). We do not identify with these secondary signals, just as we do not identify with the underlying secondary process—but the signals appear nonetheless. In addition, when we notice a Flirt we begin to walk through the doorway to another parallel world. Or when we step into and act out a dream figure, we enter into a parallel world. We can also switch into a parallel world by changing dimensions—for example, by getting to the Essence of an experience occurring in Dreamland. There are many other methods as well.

In psychology, stepping into a parallel world has typically been called "entering into an altered state of consciousness." An altered state is any state that is different from the one with which we normally identify. Many believe that special, in-depth methods are needed to enter an altered state. While this can be the case, in our experience altered states are also immediately available to us if we simply notice and embrace a parallel world occurring in the moment: for example, by amplifying one of our double signals while talking to someone, or noticing a mistake that occurs while painting or singing and unfolding the world that lies behind that "mistaken" experience.[9] It is also possible to change worlds by switching sensory channels. For example, if you are a *visually* oriented person, simply *moving* in any way that you like or *listening* to whatever sounds you hear can invoke an altered state of consciousness.

I like to think of role-playing and acting in theater as methods of stepping into parallel worlds in much the same way as a shaman steps into an altered state of consciousness. The actor and director Michael Chekhov speaks of taking on an imaginary body. He asks an actor to imagine and then step into the body of someone else and notice how that affects everything the actor does. An actor transforms into another person, emotionally and physically.[10]

Parallel Worlds in Music and Dance

The creativity inherent in switching from one world to another has only become clear to me recently, though I think this switching of worlds has been the source of my most creative inspirations. Let me share some of my experiences with this world-shifting in terms of music and dance before we go to the exercise.

I was never able to write music until I turned 40. One day after writing my first short pieces of music, I remember saying to Arny that I had a fantasy of hearing Joan Baez singing in a place of worship. Arny said, "Why not imagine what she would sing?" It may be hard to believe, but that small suggestion allowed me to jump out of my ordinary musical mind and imagine Joan Baez singing rather than me. Out of that imagination I began to hear one of the very first songs that I wrote. Actually, the song doesn't sound at all like something Joan Baez would sing, but it moved me deeply with its melody and waltz rhythm reminiscent of my Eastern European roots.

Some time later I was lying in bed one morning and thinking that I would love to compose a song. However, I had been feeling stuck trying to create music on the piano. As I lingered in bed in this half dreamy state, I wondered what it would be like to imagine the tune of a violin instead of the piano. I always loved the violin; and while my feeble attempts to play it nearly resulted in our neighbors moving away, I knew that there was something special about this instrument that could express something I felt deeply in my heart. As I let my mind wander into the vibration of the violin strings, a passionate melody popped into my head, which I then translated into a piano and violin piece. I realized that switching to the sounds and world of the violin had freed my musical imagination in a way I had not achieved by imagining or playing the piano alone.[11]

The musical puppet theater that I recently developed afforded me a similarly surprising and liberating experience. I began to create puppets and decided to listen to them create the songs, rather than the other way around! I asked each of them what they would like to sing in response to the theme "What I want to be when I grow up." One of the puppets said that he wanted to be a composer (see the photo at the beginning of the chapter). In another parallel metamorphosis, the same puppet said he wanted to be an academician!

The Academician

I'm going to be an academician
Wandering through the halls of universities!
Devouring books of every kind
With my enormous mind
Oh my future, is plain to see!

Another longed to be an artist and paint pictures on the Champs Elysee:

At a shady table on a warm sunny day
Sipping our coffee on the Champs Elysee
Oh to be an artist, to paint blue and gold
But is there really time or am I now, too old?

Everyone has thoughts or dreams about other worlds and life-times. Even Albert Einstein said,

The Artist

> If I were not a physicist, I would probably be a musician. I often
> think in music. I live my daydreams in music. I see my life in
> terms of music... I get most joy in life out of music.[12]

One day it dawned on me that while studying dance in college, I had one of my earliest experiences of parallel worlds and
creativity. My teacher had given me an assignment to choreograph
a dance in the style of a choreographer whom I admired.[13] I chose
Twyla Tharp, a very creative, contemporary choreographer. Tharp
incorporated ballet, popular dances, sports movements, and even
pop music into her dances—a combination that I would never
think of myself and which I greatly admired. When I tried to
model my choreography after hers, imagining that it was Tharp
choreographing, not me, I came up with a piece that was utterly
different from anything I had done previously. I chose a song that
was popular when I grew up—"I'm a Believer" by The Monkees—
and used baseball movements and social dance movements to create the piece. That dance was more freeing to my mind and body
than anything I had done in the realm of dance until then. It
opened up entirely new worlds for me.

What does it take to step into a parallel world? In order to
explore new worlds, we need a sacred attitude that values,

respects, and embraces worlds that lie outside of our identities. Such a sacred attitude might help us take the time to discover what it is like to live from a totally different viewpoint. In doing so we could discover the freshness and inspiration that are released as we switch from a familiar world to a new world.

Parallel Worlds and Creativity Exercise: Stepping into Someone Else

Try this exercise alone or with a partner who can guide you through the steps. During the exercise you will choose a creative medium that interests you and then imagine someone who represents that particular art form. The person you choose can be a *real* figure from today or from history (such as Pavarotti for opera singing, Shakespeare for writing, etc.) or an *imaginary* figure that pops up into your mind just now (for example, an imaginary teacher, mystic, therapist, painter, etc.).

Mr. Intensity

When I did this exercise the other day, I was surprised by the creative medium that I chose—philosophy and writing—and I focused on an imaginary mystical writer and philosopher who suddenly came to my mind, a woman who lived during the eighteenth century in Europe. I had a very creative time with it all, perhaps because this was an unusual artistic medium for me to inhabit.

Materials: During the exercise, I will ask you to allow your parallel world figure to express her- or himself through music, dance, painting, or other mediums. It will probably be difficult for you to know which materials you will need ahead of time. Perhaps you will just need a paper and pen. You certainly can't go wrong assembling paper and colors, notebooks and pens, musical instruments, paints, craft stuff, and/or clay. Or, you might simply start out doing section A of the exercise and when you come to section B, "Let Your Figure Create," take some time to find the materials that you need and continue on with the exercise.

FIND YOUR FIGURE

1. What are creative areas for you—for example, calligraphy, drawing, sculpture, poetry, music, business endeavors, writing, dance, photography, film, therapy, singing, philosophy, theater, teaching, relating to others, etc.? How do you normally go about creating in that/those area(s)?
2. Choose one area of creativity that you would like to explore and that comes to mind just now. This may or may not be an area with which you normally associate.
3. Now let a figure come to mind spontaneously that is associated with that art form. Let a real figure arise who is from today or the past, or let an imaginary figure from Dreamtime pop up just now.
4. Picture the time period and place that person lived/lives in. Describe it to yourself or to your partner. Where is that person—in a room, in a forest, on a busy street? Imagine who or what is around her or him. What is the atmosphere like—cold, dark, thickly covered with fog, crystal clear with blue skies? What kind of mood does this person have when she or he is about to act or create—solemn or ecstatic? A brooding or childlike mood?
5. Now begin to step into that figure.
   a. First feel the mood and atmosphere of that person and time.
   b. Begin to sit like her or him, feel like her or him. Let the atmosphere and mood affect the way you

breathe. Notice what your attention is like. Are you, as this person, concentrated or spacey? Disoriented or clear?

c. Make facial expressions that go along with the experience of being that person, and begin to move like her or him.

LET YOUR FIGURE CREATE

6. Now feel where your center of energy is as you enact that person. Does your center of energy feel as though it were in your eyes, in your stomach, in your legs? Get in touch with this energy and imagine and feel the energy stream from that place through your body and all the way out of your hands, head, and feet.

a. Now let this person begin to create, using any materials that you have available—write prose, give a lecture, compose a song, create a dance, paint or sculpt, etc. You might create something entirely new, or you might find that your figure begins to work on a project that you have been thinking about previously. Stay close to the feeling and atmosphere of that person as much as possible during this process. And remember, let *your figure* create, *not you!* Take time with this step.

b. When you have finished, make notes or a recording of your creation so that you can remember what you did. Give your creation a title, and write down who the author is!

c. If you have the time and inclination, translate this experience/creation into one more medium: For example, if it is a song, try to express the music in materials. If it is writing, express the words in dance, or imagine expressing the same creation in a live theater piece. If it is sculpture, imagine how to express this shape in terms of poetry or a relationship style.

d. Finally, ask yourself: If this person and/or this creation were to look back at you in your ordinary life, what would she/he/it advise you?

DISCUSS

7. Think about the following or discuss with your partner:

a. In what way is the feeling/quality/mood of that creation and/or person important for you?
b. Is there a message for you hidden within what you did? Can that message help you with your work, your relationships, your life in general?
c. How is this imagined person and the subsequent creation a *parallel* experience to your ordinary identity?
d. What was it like to translate that experience into another medium? Did doing so open up even more creative possibilities for you? How might you go further?

I hope that this exercise gave you a glimpse of the storehouse of creative energy that is connected with the act of switching from your identity into a parallel world. These worlds are present all the time; you can call on them for inspiration whenever needed, as long as you put your identity aside for a few moments to allow them to arise.

Here is a short glimpse of my experience when I became an 18th-century mystical writer and philosopher. The atmosphere was a bit gray and thick. I imagined this woman in a room with a desk, alone, very inward, moving slowly and solemnly. *She* began to write a piece of prose called "My Fragile and Enduring Place in Eternity." The beginning went something like this:

And so my hands begin to write as if propelled by a thousand ghostlike forces. And I, swept along by time, moved by the force of eternity, am utterly bound to this place where my feet rest. I sit still, as I cross the oceans and centuries.

Here in this house, on this chair, my body decays slowly. Crumbling to dust, blood mixing with bones, I dissolve from this temporary guesthouse. Perhaps I will appear again, at some time, in some place, in some other transitory hotel. Others will carry on where I left off, unaware of the breath that moves them, just as I am unaware of the invisible breath that moves me.

Oh, how I am compelled to write to you today, knowing that you may not hear me for hundreds of years; or perhaps not at all. A breeze just passed my lips. Is it the same breeze that you will feel as well?

Notes

1. Arnold Mindell, *Quantum Mind: The Edge between Physics and Psychology* (Portland, Oregon: Lao Tse Press, 2000), 234–235.
2. Arnold Mindell, *The Deep Democracy of Open Forums* (Charlottesville, Virginia: Hampton Roads, 2002).
3. Arny discusses the way in which you can solve problems in one dimension by going to a hyperspace in *Quantum Mind*, chapter 22.
4. I have also written about the connection between parallel worlds and creativity and described a number of other methods by which to step into parallel worlds. See "Amy's Hyperspaces: Creativity, the Bird of Paradise, and the Doorway to Parallel Worlds," (article on author's website, http://www.aamindell.net/research_frame.htm, 2002).
5. Michael Michalko, *Cracking Creativity: The Secrets of Creative Genius* (Berkeley, California: Ten Speed Press, 2001), 15.
6. Michalko, 15.
7. Robert Rosenblum, *Cubism and Twentieth-Century Art* (New York: Harry N. Abrams, 2001), 42. Roenblum speaks about the way in which Stravinsky expressed the human and puppet sides of Petrushka in his compositions by using polytonality, in which two different tonalities or keys are played simultaneously. He also speaks of the writings of Gertrude Stein, James Joyce, and Virginia Woolf; Joyce and Woolf were both born within a year of Picasso and Braque (founders of Cubism); their novels *Ulysses* and *Mrs. Dalloway*, respectively, span one day's time but with many parallel versions.
8. Rosenblum, 42.
9. For more on the creative use of so-called unintended or mistaken aspects of musical performance, see Lane Arye, *Unintentional Music: Releasing Your Deepest Creativity* (Charlottesville, Virginia: Hampton Roads, 2001).
10. Franc Chamberlain, *Michael Chekhov* (London: Routledge, 2004). See also Chamberlain's review of these methods in Chapter 2 of his book, where he describes the process of stepping into the independent life (or parallel world) of a character.
11. Thanks to Heike Spoddeck for playing violin on the recording of that tune.
12. G.S. Viereck, "What Life Means to Einstein: An Interview by George Sylvester Viereck." *The Saturday Evening Post* (October 26, 1929).
13. Many thanks to my dance teacher, Dimi Reber.

Chapter 10

MUSICAL PARALLEL WORLDS

Chez Noodle

Music is for me as close to the Essence as anything I know. Some things in life are as vast as the ocean and as eternal as the night sky. Playing music and singing have always brought those domains to me; they return me to a sentient home for which I long.

We have touched on the world of song and music a bit in other parts of this book, and there will be more in later chapters.[1] Here I'd like to focus on the use of sound to explore parallel worlds. In the exercise you'll notice two different sounds or rhythms that Flirt with you as you listen to a piece of music or as you listen to sounds in the environment. We'll then experiment with the relationship between these two parallel world sounds and create a musical movement phrase that connects them. The final combination will be a simple musical motif or "ideograph" (à la Julie Taymor) that can be used as the basis of a creative project.[2]

We will also see that both parallel worlds are connected with aspects of our personal processes. One of the sounds will be closer to our primary process—that is, our ordinary identity. The other will be closer to our secondary process—that is the part of our process that is further away from our identity and more unknown. These worlds are parallel and usually have very little relationship to one another. We'll explore their connection through the use of sound, movement, and drawing.

Both exercises can be done alone or with a partner to guide you.

Dancing Note

Sound, Motifs, and Parallel Worlds Exercise

Materials: During the exercise you will need to play a short piece of music, about 3 minutes long. Choose any music that you like. I tend to choose something from nature, such as the sounds of the ocean or whales, Tuva music from Mongolia, or Didgeridoo music from Australia. You will also need crayons, markers or paint, paper, and any other materials that might be useful (for example, musical instruments, fabric, etc.).

As always, follow your own experiences. If these instructions are not quite right for you, sculpt them to fit your individual process.

1. Think of a project that you are working on, for which you would like more input. Or think of a question about your life for which you would like input. Write it down.
2. Find a comfortable place to sit or lie down. Take time to stretch and be with yourself.
3. Now turn on the music.
    a. As you listen to the music, notice a sound or rhythm that catches your attention, or notice how your body already has begun to move in response to a particular sound or rhythm of the music. Focus on this sound or rhythm. Let it influence your movement as you begin or continue to move. Make your own sounds that go along with that movement, and let an image arise that mirrors that experience in some way.
    b. After a few minutes play the music again. This time, notice a second sound or rhythm that catches your attention but that you hadn't noticed before, or that might even disturb you. Let this sound or rhythm begin to express itself through your movement. Add sound and let an image come that goes with this experience. Explore and remember it.
4. Now turn off the music. Experiment with both sounds and movements.
    a. Make the first movement and sound with your body.
    b. Next, make the second movement and sound.
    c. Now go back and forth between these two movements and sounds and feel the way that they relate to one another, whether they fluidly flow into each other or are jarringly different. You might try doing

one movement after the other, perhaps using one part of the body to do one movement and then another part of the body to do the other. Continue to accompany your movement with sounds. Enjoy experimenting and let a movement phrase emerge that incorporates both in some way. Experiment with your movement phrase until the two elements find their natural path in relationship to one another and a new third phrase (and perhaps an image) emerges.

5. Now get a piece of paper and crayon, marker, or paint. Make a motion with your hands that mirrors the combined movement phrase you just created, and let your hand draw two or three strokes on your paper that represent the Essence of that phrase.

6. Now translate that simple drawing into a couple of words and write them down on your paper. You have created your own movement and musical motif.

7. Go one step further, if you like, and imagine how that dance phrase and its Essence, this motif, might express themselves in some further creative form that you imagine or on which you are currently working. For example, how might you use this motif as the basis of a creative story? How could you express and elaborate on this motif through the voices of various instruments? How could this motif be used as the basis of a theater production, a choreographed dance, sculpture, costume, song, or a piece of writing. How might this motif be used as a style of communicating in relationships?

8. Take time to consider the following:

    a. Are you aware of the original movements/sounds in the beginning of the exercise as mirroring two types of body energies that you experience throughout the day? Is one of these experiences closer to your identity than the other?

    b. How might the whole process—the combination of both movements and sounds (the final phrase and motif)—be useful in your life?

    c. Does this experience help you interpret a recent dream in some way?

Here is an example from one of the participants of my class. The first sound that this man heard in the music was a low hum. His body began to slowly curl inward, and he had the image of going into a cave. He made deep humming noises to go with this experience. The second sound/rhythm that caught his attention was a fast vibration that made his body shake quickly, as if he were cold and trying to shake off something. He had the image of a horse that was shaking off flies. He made a whooshing sound as he made the horse's motions.

When he experimented with both of these movements, he did them in succession. After some time a third experience arose: he felt as though he was a bird that dove down in the water and then rose up and shook off its feathers. As he made this movement phrase again and again, he could feel that it was an expression of first going deeply inside of himself and then letting things emerge in the world spontaneously. He drew the following picture:

Diving Inward and Rising Up

He started to create a story based on this motif. The story was about a lone hobbit who loved to cook. The hobbit went into his hobbit hole and began to create all sorts of wonderful dishes. Little did he know that the smells from his cooking emerged out of the crust of the earth, and many ordinary people began to gather around to find out where the smell was coming from. The hobbit heard the rumbling of feet above him and decided to go out and see what was happening. When he saw the people, he invited them in for a feast, and everyone enjoyed hanging around, eating, and speaking about the meaning of life.

The man had recently dreamed that he had to go on vacation for a while but that he would then come back and take part in political life. He understood this to mean that he didn't need to press himself to *be* in the world but that he could go deeply inside himself, and that his inner experiences would naturally rise up and express themselves in his worldly interactions.

Parallel Sounds in the Environment Exercise

Let's try a variation of the parallel worlds exercise. It begins by noticing a sound that Flirts with you in the environment currently surrounding you. You can do this exercise indoors or outdoors. You will recreate the sound that you heard with you own voice and then listen for a *secondary* sound *within* the first one. That means you will notice an *unintentional* sound within the first sound that you are making—something strange that doesn't quite fit or go along completely with the first sound.[3]

For example, you might notice that when you make the first sound with your own voice, you also hear a nasal sound or a cracking in your voice that doesn't quite go along with the original sound. In the exercise, I will ask you to play with these two sounds, create a musical motif from their combination, and imagine how to use this motif as the basis of some creative endeavor on which you are working.

Perhaps it will help to first give a short example. When I did this exercise the first time, I was in our kitchen and my attention was caught by the sound of the low humming of the refrigerator. I began to make the sounds myself and started to rock back and forth at the same time. I had the image of myself chanting a prayer. I then listened more closely to the sounds I was making for a secondary sound. As I made the humming sound, I also heard a slight whining or grinding sound in my voice. I expressed this grinding sound more fully. I added movements to go along with that sound: quick, forceful, linear motions with my arms and hands in all directions. As I did this I had the image of a bratty child who wanted to fight.

I played with the relationship between these two motions/ sounds, and out of that interaction came what to me was a martial-arts-type phrase: first I moved slowly and circularly with my arms and whole body, and then suddenly I made a big slashing movement with one of my arms. This is what my drawing looked like, a circle with a strong line that cut across it:

After I created the motif, I considered how I might use it as background sound for a theater piece on which I was working about the theme of war. I realized that the mixture of the two qualities expressed in musical form the clash between the force of peace and the force of war. I began to fantasize about a piece of music composed of a combination of chanting and thunder sounds.

Here are the steps of the exercise.

1. Write down a project that you are thinking about and on which you would like more input. Or just enjoy the experience, and afterward think about how it relates to your life and your creativity in general.
2. Listen to the environment. Notice an acoustical Flirt that catches your attention. If there are many, focus on the Flirt that you intuitively feel is the right one on which to focus just now.
3. Make the sound of that Flirt yourself and find the movements that go along with it. Allow an image to arise that goes along with that experience as well.
4. Next, make the original sound again and listen for a secondary unintentional sound within the first one. What sound do you hear that doesn't quite go along with the first sound? Express this unintentional sound in movement, and find an image that goes along with it.
5. Now, like a seed, plant these two experiences and play around with them in movement and sound. Let the two images and sounds interact with one another in dance and sound/singing. Let them interweave like a story that is unfolding, even if you don't know where it is going. These two experiences may melt together, or they may remain separate. Simply experiment with them. If possible, create a movement phrase that incorporates both.

Sugar Mu

6. Now get a piece of paper, express the two sound/move-ments with your hands, and then make a couple of brush strokes that describe that experience. Write a couple of words on the paper that describe this experience.
7. Imagine how this motif could help you with your creative project or, if you do not have a creative project, how it could help you with your life as a whole.
8. Think about the following: Does one of the original sounds/movements/images go along with your ordinary primary identity? Is the other sound/movement/image further away from the way you ordinarily identify your-self? How can you use them both or the combination of both in your life?

Notes

1. For an innovative discussion of the sounds that appear in our dreams and methods to work with them see playwrite, director, and psychotherapist IONE, *Listening in Dreams: A Compendium of Sound Dreams, Meditations, and Rituals for Deep Dreamers* (New York: iUniverse, 2005).

2. For an in-depth discussion of "Parallel World Songs," see see Arnold Mindell, *The Quantum Mind and Healing: How to Listen and Respond to Your Body's Symptoms* (Charlottesville, Virginia: Hampton Roads, 2004), chapter 8. Here the author explores the parallel tones and overtones in our bodies, the way in which they connect to hyperspaces, and for an exercise on the use of tones and overtones as a healing force with body symptoms. Also see Lane Arye, *Unintentional Music: Releasing Your Deepest Creativity* (Charlottesville, Virginia: Hampton Roads, 2001) for detailed descriptions and exercises on how to work with music and the creativity behind musical "mistakes." See also Pauline Oliveros, *Deep Listening: A Composer's Sound Practice* (New York: iUniverse, 2005) for numerous creative methods to work with sound and composition.

3. For an in-depth discussion of secondary sounds see Arye, *Unintentional Music: Releasing Your Deepest Creativity*, 33-36 and 103-116.

LAZY DOG

Lazy Dog and Disciplined Master, "The Boot"

P arallel Worlds turn up in so many places. Lazy Mind and Doing Mind are frequent residents of my body and mind. They are always getting into squabbles with one another, and their stalemates make it hard to move forward with my creative work, especially when the conflict is beneath the threshold of my awareness and I am unconsciously, stubbornly resisting doing something.

While creating my puppet theater I spontaneously portrayed this conflict by writing a song in which a lazy dog doesn't want to go out for *another* walk with her disciplined master. The master, The Boot, thinks the dog should get up and stop being so sluggish. The dog sings and moans to an unhurried country-western tempo:

You said I should get up and go for a walk
But all I want to do is lay here on the floor
Yeah, I know it's late, and I hate
To make you wait
So why don't you go yourself right out the door!

With a little attention and compassion for both the dog and the master, I realize that I need access to both of these energies. If I am too focused, I feel imprisoned and unable to think creatively. If I dream too much, I tend to ignore the more grounded and earthy aspects of my process. One way to do both is to do my work and, if I feel tired, to lie back and dream—while maintaining my lucid attention—catching Flirts and experiences that I can then bring back and use in my outer life.

This just happened! I was feeling lazy and didn't feel I had the energy to work on the book. I felt daunted by its many pieces and parts, and it all seemed too much for me. After much grumbling, feeling uncomfortable and tired physically, and avoiding it all by surfing the Web for a while, I took a moment to stop and focus on the Intentional Field. I felt my body lean slightly forward, and it felt as though I were pushing a big rock. The rock spoke and said I should go back to work and complete this chapter. I whined and said that I didn't want to, that it was too hard. The rock said that I had gotten to an edge, a barrier, and that if I went back and worked out the difficulties, I would feel better.

I was subtly aware that when I get to such blocks in my work and feel I can't go forward, I often start to feel achy, tired, and finally moody and distracted. It all goes downhill from there! Luckily, in this instance, I did pick myself up and go back to work, holding myself to the grindstone and completing another chapter.

I realized that I so often think that creativity has to do with the realms of music and theater and art and that it has nothing to do with "hard work!" (Not that theater and art can't be hard work as well!) From one perspective things are hard; from another, when the river is flowing down the stream of what I call hard work, it doesn't feel like hard work at all; instead it feels natural and fluid. The spontaneous flow of the Intentional Field moves in many directions, often unpredictably, and can express itself equally in the creation of a puppet or the filling out of a job application!

Anyway, that is what I did—am doing right now—and I feel a lot better! That rock wasn't such a bad character after all! Of course, you will have your own creative solution at the edge. Perhaps you need to deviate, go in a completely different direction to find your way. Maybe you need a change of attitude toward your work, a more playful one. Or maybe you have to work even more, for more hours than you had wanted. Each person and each moment is different. The most satisfying task, however, is to feel the direction that the Intentional Field is moving you in and to allow yourself to follow that stream.

Chapter 11

DREAMBODY PUPPETS

"Acid Stomach" Puppets:
Bee Wild and Auntie Acid

I n our yearly Dreambody Lava Rock Clinic on the Oregon coast, which Arny and I give together with our colleague Max Schuepbach, participants and staff join together to study and work in an intimate setting on body-symptom experiences using process oriented methods. Over the years we have explored many different kinds of bodywork and body-symptom methods to discover the messages and potential creativity within body experiences. In one of the recent clinics, Arny and I decided to apply some of my newest puppet ideas to creatively explore the dreaming experiences in our bodies.

Many of us suffer a great deal from our body symptoms and seek alternative or allopathic approaches to help relieve or heal them.[1] As process workers we consider necessary measures to relieve body symptoms as well as attempt to discover the messages within the symptom itself, assuming that the dreaming process within the symptom contains a great deal of wisdom. Puppets can help us explore the inner dimensions of our body symptoms by giving us a means of taking *a step away* from these otherwise painful and troublesome experiences and artistically exploring the energetic and creative processes within them. Hence, the birth of "Dreambody puppets"!

It has been exciting to see how quickly and easily people have taken to this task and how the mere suggestion to create some sort of puppet from body experiences has opened a door to the invention of very imaginative puppet figures. The body is an artistic canvas filled with colorful, troublesome, and wonderful puppet figures waiting to be known.

As noted previously, when the energy of the Intentional Field manifests without our conscious awareness, it can sometimes arise in the form of a disturbing body symptom. If we are able to go back to the roots of these experiences, we can get in touch with the flow of the Intentional Field *prior to* its appearance as a body symptom. In so doing, it is possible to discover a great deal of energy and potential creativity—and sometimes physical relief—hidden within those symptoms.

In this chapter, you'll find a fun and simple exercise to gain insight into the dreaming behind one of your body symptoms, whether chronic or acute, by discovering the puppet figures and Essence within it. The exercise doesn't require much psychological know-how or training. All you need is a little bit of imagination, a couple of paper plates, some crayons, and other miscellaneous materials. Or if you're in a lazy mood, forget the materials and simply use your hands to represent the puppets!

Puppets as Bridge Builders

I think everyone enjoys toys and puppets, or at least most of us did as children. Many puppets, such as the Muppets, are recognized in many countries. I think puppets speak a universal language that transcends cultural borders. Many cultures have a long history of puppetry—for example, the method of *bunraku* in Japan and the shadow puppets in Indonesia.

Puppets themselves are bridge builders; they are capable of spanning worlds and dimensions. Like Harry the Hippie, puppets can break through Consensus Reality and bring the Dreaming worlds right into our living rooms. They are a safe way of learning about ourselves because we can remain in ordinary reality, put a puppet on our hand, and quickly gain access to the dream world with its magical times, spaces, and stories—all without having to leave the comfort of our couch!

Puppets and the Puppeteer

The relationship between puppet and puppeteer is a terrific analogy for understanding the relationship of the human to the Intentional Field. When a puppeteer moves a puppet, from the puppet's point of view it is as if an unknown force has moved her, him, or it hither and thither. The same goes for humans! The Intentional Field is always subtly moving us, like puppets, though we most often don't know it is there.

In the exercise we'll get in touch with that unseen force that moves the puppets inside our body symptoms.

Body Symptoms and Dreambody
Paper Plate Puppets Exercise

In this exercise, you'll discover two puppets hidden within one of your body symptoms. Let me explain. Symptoms generally consist of two parts that are in conflict with one another. One is the part of the body that feels like the "victim" or recipient of the symptom. The other is the "symptom maker," the energy experienced as creating that symptom. Both of these are parallel worlds hidden with our aches, pains, and skin problems.

We'll use a simple method that calls on our childlike imaginations[2] to envision both aspects of our symptoms as puppet figures with their own viewpoints, clothing, expressions, hair, etc. We'll then create these puppets with the help of paper plates.

I've found paper plates to be the easiest and most useful way of creating these symptom puppets. The paper plate has more stability than a sock or other medium that we might choose, and it's easier to fasten things onto! It is most helpful to create the paper plate puppets quickly, without thinking much, because doing so ensures that you do not have too much time to ruminate about what you are doing; your puppets, then, are spontaneous creations of the moment. The rapid nature also ensures that there isn't much time for your inner critic to disturb or block your creativity.

Participant's s Paper Plate Body-Symptom Puppets

During the exercise you'll give each of your puppets a name, let them speak, and perhaps get them to sing a little song. Then you will begin a dialogue between the two puppets, attempting to find a resolution between their diverse energies. This dialogue will, hopefully, give you greater insight into the conflicting energies behind your body symptom and a potential resolution.

Finally, you will create a puppet that represents the Essence of that resolution (or, if you can't find a resolution, the Essence of the more difficult puppet figure)—that is, the most eternal aspect of your body experience.

You can do this exercise alone or with the help of a partner. If you do it with a helper and you feel stuck when you are having the puppets engage in dialogue, ask your partner to hold them up and spontaneously play out the dialogue for you. You can then sit outside, watch the theater unfold, or join in when you feel something new needs to happen.

Before starting, let me give you a hint about how this exercise might progress from my own process. (Other examples can be found at the end of the chapter.) I focused on my experience of an acid stomach. The part of my body *receiving* that symptom was my stomach. When I envisioned my stomach as a type of puppet, I imagined a soft and happy, round figure who I named Auntie Acid. I called her this because of her similarity to the effects of antacid medication! Auntie Acid had a big, wide, spacey sort of smile on her face. When she moved, she rolled around slowly like a ball, gently, softly, and happily singing "Rolling, rolling, in and out, nothing to do and nothing to doubt!"

I imagined the *symptom maker*, the one *creating* the stomach pain, as an intense, fiery, and pointed critical character whom I called Bee Wild. His face and eyes were angular and full of bright colors; his movements were jagged and pointed. To my surprise he sang the beginning of Beethoven's Fifth in a sort of menacing way, "Da, da, da, da daaaaaaa!!!"

I created these two figures with paper plates and let them dialogue with one another. (See the picture of Bee Wild and Auntie Acid at the beginning of this chapter.)

Though they disagreed about almost everything—Auntie Acid approached life in a fun and easygoing sort of way, and Bee Wild wanted to be more direct and intense—they did come to a resolution together. They decided that it was okay to put their energies together: to be first sharp and then easy-going. The Essence of that resolution, its seed before it became so sharp and so easygoing, was the experience of having an empty mind that would suddenly burst out in spontaneous acts, only to retreat back to an empty, quiet place. When I imagined this Essence as a humanlike figure, I envisioned a Zen meditator. I later created my own rendition of this figure in greater form out of newspaper and other materials:

My Zen Meditator Puppet

Now, lets try the exercise.

Materials: You will need three paper plates and some markers or crayons with which to draw. Any other fun materials, such as feathers, fabric, or tissue, can be helpful. Again, you may not know what materials you will need until you begin to create the puppet. You can search for them at that point. Again, if you do not want to use paper plates, you can simply act out these puppets with your hands.

Alone
1. Choose a symptom you can feel now or have felt in the past.
2. Identify the area of body that is affected—that is, the area that is receiving the trouble.
   a. Imagine a puppet that could represent and play that body part. How would it look? What facial expression, hair, shape, and colors would it have? How would it move? What is its energy like?
   b. Use a paper plate as the base and create this puppet/ figure in your own creative way. For example, draw it, color it, add fabric or pieces of grass, curl, twist, or tear the plate. When you are finished, give it a name

and write that name on the back of your plate. Play with this puppet and discover how it speaks, moves, or even sings.

Theresa's Body-Part Puppet

3. Now feel the energy of the *symptom maker*, the symptom creator. Express this energy with your hands and face.
   a. Now imagine a puppet that could represent that symptom maker. How would it look? What facial expression, hair, shapes and colors would it have? How would it move? What is its energy like?
   b. Use a paper plate to create that puppet/figure. Give it a name and write that name on the back of your plate. Play with it and discover out how it speaks, moves, and sings.

Heike's Symptom-Maker Puppet

Alone or with a partner

4. If you have a partner, share your two paper plate figures with her or him. Show your partner the types of movements, rhythms, or songs that go along with the puppets. Or do this alone, holding both plates up yourself.

Kanae's Puppet Dialogue

5. Have your two paper plate puppets begin to dialogue.
   a. Play both sides yourself, or hold and act out one figure while your partner acts out the other. You can also switch back and forth.
   b. Let the two puppets dialogue with one another until they find a resolution in the puppet world. If you can't find a satisfying resolution, skip to 6b.

Lily and Vassiliki Dialoguing with Puppets

6. Now get to the Essence in one of two ways:
   a. If you were able to get to a resolution, find its
      Essence. That is, express with hand motions the reso-
      lution you found . Now, make the same movement
      you just made with your hands again, but this time
      more slowly, still feeling the same intensity and
      energy—and continue to do it even more slowly until
      you feel the seed or root of that experience. Express
      this Essence with a couple of words.
   b. If you were unable to get to a satisfying resolution,
      get to the Essence of the *more difficult* figure. Choose
      the figure that is more difficult or complex for you,
      and put the other puppet to the side. Express the
      energy of this difficult figure with your hands. Now
      make the same motion more slowly, until you feel the
      seed or root of that energy. Express this Essence with
      a couple of words.
7. Now imagine a third puppet/figure that could represent
   that Essence; it might be human, animal, or a piece of the
   natural world.
   a. Using another paper plate as your base (or any other
      materials) create that Essence in any way that you
      like. When you are finished, write the name of this
      Essence on the back of your plate or materials.

Tamara's Essence Puppet

b. When you are done creating this figure, sit with it for a moment. Let it make movements, sounds, or a song. Perhaps it will speak to you (and your partner) about itself and will teach you how to be in that state as well.

c. When you have a good sense of the quality of that Essence figure, put your paper plate creation down and become this Essence figure yourself for a few minutes. Sit like it, move like it, feel like it, and imagine the kind of lifestyle it suggests.

8. Integration:

a. Try to feel this Essence experience in your symptom area and notice its effects. Feel it in your whole body and notice how this feels.

b. Imagine how to live this Essence in everyday life, at your work, in relationships, and how it can help you with your creative work.

c. Make notes about your experience.

Here are some helpful questions to consider after completing the exercise:

• How has this experience been trying to happen in some way in your life? For example, have you experienced it in your body? In your relationships? In your creativity? In your dreams?

• Can you sense/tell how the final Essence integrates both parts of your symptom, both puppets?

This exercise may have helped you realize that if the Essence and Intentional Field are marginalized, they tend to appear in dualistic figures that are troublesome or at least antagonistic to one another. In this case, you experience two antagonistic forces within your body symptoms. It's natural to have opposing forces and to have body symptoms. But getting to the Essence behind these figures can relieve your symptoms as well as give you access to important information and a good deal of creativity.

Here are a couple of short examples of people's experiences with this exercise. At the end of the exercise, some of the individuals created Essence puppets, some drew the Essence, and others simply experienced it.

Beauty and the Beast

A woman worked with her difficulties with breathing. Ever since she was a child, she has had trouble with her respiratory system, specifically her bronchial tubes and lungs. As a child she was always very sick with asthma and once nearly died; she went out of her body due to the inability to breathe.

For the area of her lungs and bronchia she imagined a romantic, innocent girl who is a little scared but who believes in goodness and thinks that the world is basically good. Her symptom-maker puppet was a mean-looking monster. The little girl is afraid of him and runs away and hides, but the monster keeps pursuing her. He roars and threatens her.

Beauty   *Beast*

What was the resolution? The little girl hid so many times that the monster became very lonely. At the same time, the little girl felt that life didn't have much color without him. She longed for the monster's passion and colorfulness. After finally meeting and having a good discussion, the little girl became aware of her warm feelings for the monster. Actually, they realized that they loved each another. (The woman realized that this was very much like the story of Beauty and the Beast.) Finally the resolution she found was a combination of the little girl's loving care and the monster's passion. It was *compassion*! The Essence figure that she created was a heart full of light and colors, and this made her very happy.

Compassion

Easy Winds and Iron Man

Another woman also worked on her asthma, a tightness and stiffness in the breast region. The puppet that represented her chest area was called Easy Winds. Easy Winds is not easy to grasp and is kind of soft and windy and spacey and has a quiet energy. Her voice has a dreamy quality, detached and peaceful. The symptom-maker puppet was Iron Man; he is very intense and his body is tight. He speaks in clear, short sentences. He is demanding, confronting, and fearless.

Easy Winds   *Iron Man*

Easy Winds and Iron Man didn't find a satisfactory resolution, so the woman tried to get to the Essence of the more difficult figure, Iron Man. When she made his angular and demanding motions in a slower manner, she found the seed of that experience: a crystal that is very focused and centered. This crystal is able to grasp the truth and wisdom of the moment. She drew this crystal on a piece of paper. The figure representing the Essence was a Zen master who banged a huge gong and was deeply connected with his inner life and wisdom while being attached and detached at the same moment.

Crystal

Hard Shell Outside, Soft Inside

A man I worked with spoke about feeling that he didn't know what to do with his life and that he was frequently afraid of the world. He said that he had a chronic sore throat. For the area of the throat, he created a puppet out of a long tube of flowing polka-dotted fabric, put two feathers for eyes, and a flower on top. He said this puppet had a very loose, soft, way of going about life.

The symptom creator, on the other hand, was a tough, nasty man with big shoulders, wide hips, big muscles, and hands that looked like claws. He had a nasty scowl on his face and looked like he was ready to get in a fight. He wore a flannel shirt that wasn't tucked in at the bottom. To simplify things he created a puppet of the clawing hand. (See both figures on the next page.)

When these two puppets interacted with one another, the neck puppet flowed around loosely and aimlessly. The clutching pup-

Throat   Symptom Creator

pet grabbed the neck puppet with his hand and started to crush it and squeeze it. The neck puppet squealed and said, "What are you doing to me?" The clutching puppet said, "You have no form! You have to get tougher!" The neck puppet replied, "But I'm not tough, I'm flowing!" The clutching puppet said, "You need to get firmer inside! Go inside yourself and get in contact with yourself. You are too related to the outside!"

At that point, this man had a revelation. He realized that he tends to be very nice to people and looks to others for affirmation about himself. Because of that, he experiences a good deal of insecurity in life. He tended to look more outside than inside for his sense of himself. Realizing the resolution, he said that he needed to spend more time focusing on himself inwardly. He expressed this feeling by closing his eyes, raising his hands in the air to his sides, then slowly bringing them inward to his chest.

He said this experience was very close to the Essence, but that he would like to try to go a step deeper. He made the motion again with his arms, then in slower and slower motion until he felt the seed behind it. He said he felt as if he were a piece of fruit or squash that had a hard outer shell and was soft inside—a soft, inward focus, yet surrounded by an outer protective surface toward the world. To represent this Essence, he used a squash and drew two closed eyes on it (see photo). He realized that this figure brought together the energies of his two earlier puppet figures, softness and toughness.

Squash Essence

Spinning in Silence

Sara experienced bouts of dizziness because of Meniere's disease, a disturbance of the inner ear characterized by periodic episodes of vertigo or dizziness, intermittent low-frequency hearing loss, a loud ringing in the ears, and a sensation of pressure in the ear.

Sara chose the head as the symptom receiver, but quickly this head turned into a brain that flounced around the room saying in a deep voice, "I am Sara's brain, and I like to think complicated thoughts!" The symptom maker was a carnival barker who turned the Sara's brain upside down and spun it around one of the centrifugal rides that had scared her when she was a child. When the two figures began to dialogue with one another, the carnival barker sneered at the brain and said, "Sweetheart, you're too much! I'm going to turn you upside down and inside out!" "No, no! I like to be straight and clear!" said the brain. The carnival barker continued, "Oh you do, do you? Well, here's a spin!" After arguing for a while, the brain stood upside down, and the barker was pleased.

Head and Brain   *Carnival Barker*

While the brain was upside down, Sara had the sense of silence around her. This felt like the Essence to her, a deep sense of quietness, and she imagined an Essence figure, someone spinning in space in utter silence. (See drawing below.)

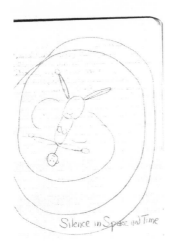

Spinning Silently in Space

Presence

Heike, a woman in her late twenties, has multiple sclerosis. After a year of good health, her health was now going downhill once again. She was feeling acutely exhausted and had a lot of trouble walking. She did not make puppets but adapted this exercise in the form of imagining the music her puppets would play. She chose to focus on her physical sense of exhaustion, amplified by a head-ache.

Heike said that the symptom was in her whole body but that the area that suffered the most in the moment was her upper body and head. She imagined a puppet that would represent this area of her body as "really depressed and playing a sad tune on the piano."

She imagined the symptom maker as a wild puppet who was hitting the depressed one. In terms of music, she imagined this puppet hitting a huge cymbal, making lots of noise. Heike stood up and acted this out, hitting her hands together and making a lot of sound. (She said it was actually a lot of fun to do that, especially being so loud!)

When the two parts began to dialogue together, she hummed the first sad tune and then made the loud crashing cymbal sounds. The two sounds began to merge and transformed into a tune filled with deep and low piano tones that slowly became louder and more intense.

She tried to get to the Essence of that music, its original spark. She discovered the figure of Mother Teresa who said, "Bring out the suffering Illness. Relate to the suffering. Talk about the suffering. Don't forget it." Heike explained that Mother Teresa always looked at suffering and never looked away. She said: "In that moment when I thought of Mother Teresa, I felt incredibly present. I feel as though there is no gravity. Every atom in my body is just there, where it is. It's amazing. Also, I have the sense of a kind of willpower and I'm very focused."

Heike said that frequently, when she is not feeling well, she either doesn't talk about her feelings of unwellness to others or she downplays them. However, she realized that if she does talk about what she is experiencing, it feels good, is relieving, and she is less likely to ignore and run over her physical limitations. At the same time, others listen and do not ignore her suffering (or their own).

"This goes along with the feeling of being incredibly present," Heike said. "Like being present in all that I am, not just the nice, happy parts, but the parts in pain and the parts that feel hopeless as well. And then I'm fully there. I am just who I am. I don't try to hide that I'm different, handicapped, and what have you. I feel like there is no gravity and therefore no exhaustion. In a way the symptom is gone, but kind of by not going away. I know this doesn't quite make sense, but this is how it feels. I can just be."

Heike imagined the final music that would go along with her Essence experience. It was a whole orchestra with a huge drum playing a tune in D minor, which gets louder and louder. She called it The Big Noise. We can see how this Essence experience brings the earlier two puppets together. One is sad and in pain; the other is loud and expressive. She realized that it is a relief to talk about her suffering to others.

Notes

1. For an example of the use of dance, visualization, art, and guided meditation for healing, see Anna Halprin, *Dance as a Healing Art* (Kentfield, California: Tamalpa Institute, 1997).

2. This is a simple method that does not require the ability to focus on sensory-grounded information, which is another type of process-oriented symptom work. You can read about this type of work in Arnold Mindell, *Working with the Dreaming Body* (London, England: Penguin-Arkana, 1984. Reprint. Portland, Oregon: Lao Tse Press, 2002); and Joseph Goodbread, *The Dreambody Toolkit: A Practical Introduction to the Philosophy, Goals and Practice of Process-Oriented Psychology* (2d ed. Portland, Oregon: Lao Tse Press, 1997). For an overview of Process Work, see Max Schuepbach, "Process Work," In *Handbook of Complementary and Alternative Therapies in Mental Health*, edited by S. Shannon, 355-373 (San Diego: Academic Press, 2002).

Part IV

CRITICS AND BIG ENERGY

The bee was buzzing
Buzz, swat, buzz
Bugging and criticizing me
Till I looked closer
To see what it was
A raging figure
Full of colors, energy, and might
Couldn't I use its intensity to create
Instead of enduring yet another
Miserable night?

Chapter 12

IT'S ALL A BUNCH OF JUNK!

Mr. Square

W ell, in all fairness, this book should have a section solely devoted to critics, incessant mean voices, and miscellaneous beings who tend to criticize and put a halt to our creative work, not to mention unidentifiable blocks and impasses that can be a real misery! I don't think I've ever met anyone who doesn't have at least a doubtful voice now and then that enters the sanctum of her or his eardrum. Don't you wish they would just go away and leave you alone? Wouldn't life be much better? But hey, isn't this a democracy? Maybe it's better to invite them in and see what they might have to offer.

Through a lot of grief and experimentation, I've found that these difficult creatures *also* carry the seeds of the Intentional Field. Even the nastiest critics contain a tremendous amount of energy.[1] In fact, I must admit that many of my critics have been the source of some of my most inventive and zany creations. Just think of all the power they have *over you* and what you could do if you could cull that energy and use it as a creative rocket to boost you into further dimensions of the imagination.

My most consistent critic, whom I can always rely on to come around, is a rather square and uptight rationalist who tells me that I am not accomplishing enough and that what I do is not *real* enough. That's him, in the photo above. He's *very* square and extremely photogenic! He tells me all the time, "You are such a dreamer! You should put your feet *on the ground* instead of flying in the sky!" He has been the source of some of my greatest uncertainty and most unbearably blocked moments. (Or is it days or weeks?)

An inner critic can really spoil a good thing. Imagine you are enjoying your creative work, and suddenly an insistent, doubting voice sneaks up and says, "What is this? It's no good!" Sound familiar? A real wet blanket.

Many artists describe those moments of doubt and fear and have various strategies to deal with them. For example, in her book *The Creative Habit* choreographer Twyla Tharp speaks about these "mighty demons" that can shut down our creative impulses by infiltrating our thoughts so that we find ourselves worrying that—

- People will laugh at me.
- Someone has done it before.
- I have nothing to say.
- I will upset someone I love.

- Once executed, the idea will never be as good as it is in my mind.[2]

Tharp has her own creative method of critic resolution, in which she combats the fears by confronting and answering them one by one, "like a boxer looking his opponent right in the eye before a bout."[3]

Since we rarely seem to get around these demons, let's spar with their energy and make it useful. In fact, we'll discover that within these figures lies the Intentional Field and its almost imperceptible flow.

Sparring with the Critic's Energy

Discovering the Critic's Creativity Exercise

You can use the following exercise if you are feeling blocked in your creative work, or if you would like to investigate an earlier time when you felt blocked in your creativity. Perhaps you abandoned your project, or grit your teeth and suffered through it with the critic on your back.

During the exercise you will act out the critic and then get to its Essence or seed. The Essence question is: what was it before it became such a big critic? You may be surprised at what lies at the very seed of that miserable character. It will probably be very different from the critic's original form.

For example, I made an image of one of the critics that was disturbing me the other day. She was a tough gangster figure with a cigarette falling out of her mouth. She had long stringy hair, beady eyes, and a nasty, tough demeanor. She walked with a heavy rhythmic bounce and an air of certainty. She said she'd give me a lot of trouble if I didn't do what she said. Instead of giving in, I decided to step into her energy and find the Essence behind her. As I strutted around with toughness and certainty, I could feel her Essence. Shedding her outer form, I felt her root or core as a sense of great intensity and passion. I went downstairs to my piano and let that force pour out through my fingers and out came some very exciting songs that consumed me for a couple of hours!

Materials: You can do this exercise alone or with a partner's help. You will need a piece of paper and something with which to draw. In addition, you might use clay, objects from nature, or musical instruments to express the Essence. Don't worry if you do not have the materials in the beginning. Once you have found the Essence, *it* will choose what medium to use to unfold the process further, and you can then gather them.

1. Think of a time that you have wanted to be creative in your life either in your profession, in art, therapy, writing, etc., but felt blocked. If the block is happening now, focus on this moment. Perhaps you feel (or felt) that you are not creative, that your work is boring or too childish, or that nothing will come of it.

2. Imagine something that is against your creativity. What sort of figure would it be? Look at that figure in great detail in your mind's eye. What does it look like? How short or tall is it? What body shape does it have? How wide or narrow is it? What is its age? What hair color does it have? What kind of clothes would it wear? Where does it live? What tone of voice would it have? What does this figure want? How does it walk?

3. Make a quick sketch of this figure on your paper.

4. Now step into this figure. Feel it in your body, make a face like it, sit like it, walk around like this figure, make its gestures, and speak like it. Really get into the feeling of being that critic and notice the rhythm with which it moves.

Skeleton Critic

5. Inhabit that figure even more by saying words that go
   with the feeling, movement, and rhythm of the critic. Perhaps you will create a short poem or sing a little tune.
   Continue to unfold this experience in any way that you
   like. Notice how much energy it has!
6. Now get to the Essence of that figure.
   a. To do that, try using micromovements. That is, make
      the movements of the figure once again. Now put
      your arms down and recall the energy of that figure.
      Begin to recreate those motions, and just as you begin
      to move, notice the flickering experiences that you
      have; notice the first, slightest feelings and experi-
      ences just as you begin to recreate that energy. Feel
      this early flicker, its root, the place from which it
      arises. Trust your experiences and intuitions, even if
      they seem irrational, for they are its Essence.
   b. Imagine this Essence in terms of a piece of nature
      such as a rolling river, a glacier, a cave.
   c. Now assume a position/posture that expresses that
      Essence. Stand or sit like that Essence, feel it, and
      make a sound that goes with it.
   d. Unfold that Essence further. For example, look
      around your room or outside in the environment,
      and let your imagination choose objects that would

help to bring that Essence to life in material form. Perhaps it's a rock, a tube of toothpaste, or a can of corn! Or let that Essence express itself further in movement, music, poetry, writing, or relationships.

   e. Imagine how you could use this Essence energy in your life and in your creative work/projects.

7. Make notes about this critic who was troubling you and the process you went through to get to its Essence. In what way is this critic needed in terms of your momentary block or previously blocked creative path?

You may have noticed that there is a lot of energy in the critic when you enter into it consciously. Instead of draining your energy, it has a lot of fuel to give.

One businessman that I worked with complained that he just couldn't get enough of his work done. He felt that his work would never be good enough and though he worked harder and harder to "make it better," he seemed to get nowhere. He was often very tired. He imagined a critic with a pointy chin and beady eyes who taunted him and told him that his work would never be first-rate. When he acted out this critic, he stood very tall, his head was raised high, and he looked downwards in a demeaning way toward his ordinary self.

When I asked him to find the Essence of that state, the man relaxed and began to make tiny movements toward becoming that critic. His back started to straighten upwards ever so slightly, and he had a flickering feeling of pride. He translated this experience into the image of a tree that stood tall in the mountains. As he stepped into being that tree, he felt a sense of pride and centeredness with which he rarely identifies. From this state of being, he imagined that he could complete his work with a renewed sense of purpose and energy. Later on he placed a stick that he found as he was walking home next to his desk to reminded him of this experience.

The basic idea is that if something continually bothers you—if you can't get away from it no matter how hard you try—it is an important path that is asking to be unfolded. In its ordinary form it is troublesome, but at its Essence it is a deep and meaningful part of you that wants to be lived and expressed and can even bring fresh impulses to your creative work.

Tree in the Mountains

Notes

1. For an in-depth discussion of the inner critic, see Sonja Straub, "Stalking Your Inner Critic: A Process-Oriented Approach to Self-Criticism" (Unpublished thesis, Research Society for Process Oriented Psychology, 1990).
2. Twyla Tharp, *The Creative Habit: Learn It and Use It for Life* (New York: Simon & Schuster, 2003), 22.
3. Tharp, 22.

Chapter 13

MOODY MISERY

Okay, we tried to work with the critic. That's all well and good. But what if you find yourself in such a heavy mood and feel so blocked that you can't figure out what is going on or even who is criticizing or disturbing you? Has that ever happened to you? Remember when you felt utterly blocked and lost and didn't have a clue as to what was troubling you? Maybe you didn't even feel that bad—you were just stuck. Or maybe you felt so bad that you couldn't talk to anyone and just sat and hemmed and hawed all by yourself. The following are two simple exercises that will, hopefully, find some fluidity and creativity within these moods. One has to do with music, the other with puppet figures.

Musical Moods Exercise

Some moods are really miserable, and some are just bland—but every mood has a hidden song. Even if you hate music, there is some grumbling, rumbling, or monotone sound hidden in your mood that is just waiting to escape from your lips. In fact, one of the very first methods I used for writing musical tunes was to let the sound of my mood show me the way.

Luckily, this little exercise is very easy and only takes a few minutes. If you are in a mood, you certainly don't want to take much time dawdling with an exercise! Oh, don't worry if you feel you can't make music. The Intentional Field does all the work!

1. Notice your momentary mood; any mood will do.
2. Make a sound that goes with that mood; make it louder and listen to its tone.
3. Now imagine some figure or character that would go along with that sound. Do you see the Phantom of the Opera? A warthog? A sleepy dog?
4. Continue making the sound as you imagine the figure, and let the sound begin to extend itself into a little song or tune, even if it is very silly.
5. Sing this song or tune to yourself, move a little bit to it, and find out what that tune and figure are expressing or what feeling it creates. Now comes the big question: how might that information be helpful to you?

One person I worked with felt blocked in his work as a therapist. He was shy to admit that he was feeling a bit bored with his work and didn't look forward to going to the office anymore. He wasn't feeling all that bad about it, just blocked and a bit frustrated. When I asked him to make a sound that represented his mood, he surprised himself by making a sort of childlike sound that had a bouncy rhythm. As he made the sound, he imagined the cartoon figure of the Pink Panther dancing around like a wily trickster. The sound unfolded further into a sort of boogie-woogie tune. As the man sang this tune, he bopped up and down and smiled and said that he felt like a playful child. He realized that he had gotten a bit too serious in his work and needed a more lighthearted attitude with his clients.

One evening I also discovered a child hidden within my moodiness. I was trying to prepare a class that I was going to give the following week, but I felt too tired to work on all the details that it entailed. I felt frustrated and kind of grumbly. In order to express this mood, I made a grinding sort of sound with my voice and imagined an infuriated child who didn't want to have any responsibility and who just wanted to play! I began to act like this wild kid, stomping around, making mean faces, and began singing the following bratty tune:

I'm gonna be a kid to the day I die
Cause I want the freedom to scream and cry!
I'm gonna spill my milk and make a mess
And you know me, I'll never confess!
It's a bad bad world when you have to be
A grown up who acts with grace and dignity
What a bunch of junk and hype
I'd rather be the mischievous trickster type!
So give me my toys I want 'em now
Or you know who will begin to howl!
Gimme, gimme, it's all mine
I want it all, all the time!

Overgrown Kid

Well, that kid really gave me a lot of energy, and I began to plan the class with a greater sense of freedom and creativity. When I gave the class the following week, I felt more vibrant and spontaneous than normal. I was less attached to my notes and more attached to the spontaneous creativity that arose inside of me as I taught. The class felt much more alive for me and, I like to think, for the participants as well!

Moods and Puppet Figures

Exercise

For some reason, imagining moods as puppets is one of the easiest and fastest routes to Dreamland. Here is one more short method for working with your moods, in which you have only to imagine your mood in the form of a puppet. Hopefully, this magical exercise will help you turn a static, miserable mood into a river of creative potential.

Tied Up in Knots

1. Feel the mood you are in. What is it like?
2. Imagine a puppet that could represent that mood.
3. What would it wear? What kind of facial expression would it have? How big would it be?
4. Now watch that puppet in your mind's eye and imagine what it does. What kind of motions would it make? What would it say or shout?
5. Find out what it is expressing and help it unfold itself by encouraging it to express everything. Get that figure to really say what it needs and what it is really longing for. For example, some critics really want to get to the bottom of some deep issue. Some just want love and appreciation that they never got, and therefore have become moody because of their absence. Others want more influence or more fun in life. If your puppet is shy or becomes blocked in its expression, encourage it to go further—and assure it that you are listening and want to know its deepest desires.
6. Dialogue with that puppet about how you might help it reach this desire and try to come to some resolution that is satisfying for both of you.

The other day I was feeling moody and irritable and unsatisfied with my writing. I imagined my mood as a very down-to-earth truck-driver puppet who insisted that my writing and ideas about creativity were just "fairy stuff." Hmm, this pattern seems to be repeating itself! In any case, this truck driver just drives, loads, unloads, drinks coffee, eats hamburgers, and drives some more. He said:

I'm a truck driver
I drive all day and all night
I just drive this truck
And once in a while get in a fight

The other drivers drive me crazy
But I'm the commander of this deal
And I eat a hamburger and fries
At every single meal

I pick up a load
And haul it around
I'm tough and macho
And really on the ground

Not like these flakes
Who play music and sing songs
They have no feet, no meat, no muscle
They're just airy-fairy and wrong

I got to put them in order
I want to put them on the ground
Make them get it all firm
Safe and fit and sound

When I dialogued with him, I realized that he was longing for the Dreaming to be really concrete. He encouraged me to really put my feet down and show how the Intentional Field is part of everyday life and how people could actually live from day to day in interaction with it rather than just dream about it. This input has helped me to stay close to my deepest feelings about this book and about creativity; my inner truck driver has helped me to ground my ideas *concretely and firmly*. All of life becomes more generative and creative, not just those moments when we are swept up in creative inspiration.

Chapter 14

Making a Mess

A Mess

One of the worst possible moods you can get into comes from feeling like you *should* make something really good—something beautiful, artistic, special, or meaningful. What pressure! Let's take the pressure off for a while.

Since we're coming toward the end of the book, wouldn't it be relieving to *not have to be creative?* Why not just forget it all for a while—or even do something really bad, ugly, unartistic, even disgusting? It's only fair to give this mood some space here. In fact, why not make a big mess?

Exercise

1. Please make the most "uncreative," stupid, ridiculous thing with any materials that you want. For example, take a piece of paper and a crayon and make the worst drawing you could ever make—the least artistic sketch in the world! Just make sure that it is really "ugly," "dumb," or "meaningless"! Feel the energy you use as you do this.
2. Look at your creation and see if you can feel just like it feels. Make faces that go with it and become this awful thing; let it voice its opinion or tell a story.
3. If you have a friend around, share your stories with each other. Notice the relief that this brings! Don't worry about integrating what just happened; just enjoy the freedom of "not being creative"!

Sticky Tape

Speaking of messes and junk, did you ever try to wrap a present or package but kept losing the beginning of the roll of tape and had to scratch at the roll endlessly to find the beginning again? As you valiantly go further, it all becomes an even bigger mess than when you started? Such moments can turn a seemingly innocent and simple task into an infuriating one! Here's a little poem I wrote when I was wrapping a present a few months ago. I was so frustrated I decided I could at least use the energy to write a silly poem!

Sticky Tape

I took out the tape
To seal up the box
But when I pulled on the roll
It suddenly stuck to my watch!

I tried to neatly unstick it
But it got even worse
This increasingly chewy, unruly, mass of gunk
Was now sticking to my purse

I tried to pull it off
But it clung on tight
"One more pull" I muttered bravely
And yanked it with all my might

Oh, it got away
Taking half the fabric in its wake
The sticky parts were now spotted red
And it was all matted, twisted, and caked

Parts wound around other parts
Big globs and skinny strands
This lurking mass stuck to whatever it neared
Including now, my hands

"Now I'm really mad," I thought
And (unlike me) began to shout
"You stupid piece of tape!
Why didn't you just slide right out?!"

I decided to be a warrior
And win this ugly war
I prepared myself for battle
And was sure I would endure

By the time it was all over
I lay exhausted and weak
I was enveloped in the sticky stuff
From my head to my feet

The moral of the story
Is now easy to see
The gift I thought I was sending
Turned out to be me!

Chapter 15

THE SIMPLE PATH

Snow Path

B efore turning toward the end of the book, let me introduce one more thought about working with creative blocks.

Moment-to-Moment Signals

A basic Process Work concept is that everything we need is here right now; it lies in following the details of your own awareness. Simply notice what you are experiencing and follow it. If you are feeling blocked and nothing else seems to work, you can always rely on your awareness to reveal the path in which the river is flowing. It's the easiest path that I know of, and it is always at your disposal.

What is it that we notice? When the Intentional Field arises in Dreamland and Consensus Reality, it expresses itself through sensory-grounded signals such as visual images, sounds, feelings, and movements. Following these signals means noticing if you are hearing something, feeling something, seeing something, or sensing movement in your body and then helping these experiences to unfold by amplifying them and discovering their messages.

Let me tell you about my own experience. One evening a few months ago when we were in the mountains, I was feeling upset. I couldn't concentrate and wanted to *be creative*! Nothing I knew seemed to work. Hey, I'm writing a book about creativity, shouldn't I *be* creative? My stomach was in knots, I was sweating and pushing myself to do things, and I felt like a failure. Something in me said, "Just follow what you are experiencing. Notice it. Just say to yourself, 'I am aware of this, I am aware of that.' Then unfold what emerges."

I decided to follow this advice. I first noticed that I felt drawn to get up and go and sit near the windows to look out at the mountains in the late afternoon. Sunset occurs much earlier in the mountains than the city, and the sky was beginning to darken. It was a beautiful sight, but when I sat by the window, my attention was drawn to my stomach that felt as though it was tied up in knots. "Stomach clenched up," I said to myself. I then noticed my head was beginning to fall backward slightly. "Head moving backward, mouth opening. Just notice and follow what is happening, even amplify it a bit," I told myself.

I amplified this head and mouth posture by letting my head fall back a bit further. My mouth began to open slightly, and I had a sudden flickering feeling that I was a little bird chirping for its mother to feed it. I noticed my mind interpreting this, "I need spiritual feeding. I am blocked in my creativity."

Something told me that it was too early to interpret. I had not given the experience enough time to unfold. I returned to my head and mouth position and my image unfolded further. I imagined a mother bird putting a worm in my mouth and flying away. Where did she go? I tried to follow in my imagination as the mother bird flew just over the tops of the mountains. My attention was so drawn to this mother that I allowed myself to shapeshift into her and imagine it was I flying over those mountains. What an amazing feeling I had, gliding up so high in the sky!

At that moment I began to hear a faint song. I listened, trying to remember all of the sounds that drifted through me. I got up and went over to my piano and played what I was hearing. Something in me said, "Oh, gee, that begins like all the rest of my music. Change it! And besides, it's too simple." I could have stayed with that critic, but I decided that I might be at an *edge*—that is, that I had not allowed the previous experience to unfold to completion and that I should stay with it a bit longer. As I played the music, the following words flowed out of me:

A little bird is chirping
In the cold winter air
She's crying for her mother
Whose flown off somewhere

Mama's on the mountain top
Looking down from so far away
To the lake beneath her
Where her baby prays

And oh how the night comes
It takes the child by surprise
Out here in blue-gray
Winter skies

The moon appears before her
Was it there a moment ago?
It's shining like a river
A far and distant glow

It's calling out to her
With a smile that lights the night
Guiding her through the nameless path
And holding her so tight

And oh how the night comes
It takes the child by surprise
Out here in blue- gray
Winter skies

I called it "Winter Skies." It suddenly dawned on me that this song reminded me of my mother, who had died recently, and my longing for her spirit. I realized that the anguish I was experiencing with my work was connected to not feeling inwardly supported; a sense that my mother was not here anymore. I felt like a lonely child needing a guide to help show her the next step. I knew that the moment I had become that mother bird, I was beginning to get in touch with that loving support for which I longed.

At that moment I noticed myself looking once again out of the window. The sky had become much darker and, to my surprise, the moon had risen over the mountaintops and was now shining into my eyes. I felt immediately comforted, embraced by nature, by the moon with its great guiding light in the dark sky. I felt that the moon was a mother for me, an escort in the night when I do not know the way. I stayed with this feeling and felt that I could go back to my work. Rather than showing me a specific path, my process gave me what I longed for: the sense of being comforted and centered in nature, which would guide and sustain me through this work.

Moon

Simple Path Exercise

I hope that the following exercise will also be helpful to you in those moments when you feel blocked and cannot seem to find the road that lies ahead of you.

Simply use your awareness to notice what's happening. In order to unfold the process further, you can amplify experiences by "switching channels"—that is, by allowing your experience to express itself more fully in various modalities. For example, if you are seeing something, try feeling it in your body. If you are hearing something, try to express that sound in movement.

Remember that you may get to an edge as you follow your own process; that is, an impasse that emerges when you have not allowed an experience to complete itself fully. The edge refers to the boundary between our known world and other unknown experiences. When we come to the edge, we may feel lost, or our minds may begin to drift off and become unfocused, or a critical voice may interrupt what we are doing. If you notice any of these happening, it is helpful to go back to the experience you were having just before the impasse occurred. If you try a few times but are unable to complete your experience, investigate what is happening at the edge. If it's a critical voice, unfold this voice and find out what it has against your experience; a dialogue between you and it can be very helpful. Or use any other methods in the last chapters.

1. Take a moment to notice what you are experiencing. Are you seeing something, hearing something, feeling something, or do you notice movements happening in your body?

2. Focus on that thing which you notice even more. Amplify what you experience by seeing the vision more clearly, hearing the sounds more intently, feeling what you feel more powerfully, or making the movements a bit more.

3. Now switch channels to unfold your experiences even further. If you like, create a story from your experiences and ask yourself how the message of that story might be helpful to you in some way.

4. If you get to an impasse—to an edge where you feel blocked or something doubts your process—go back and try to complete what you were doing before the doubt came. If doubts continually return and you can go no further, unfold the critical voice and try to find out its deeper message. (See the "Discovering the Critic's Creativity" exercise on page 202, in Chapter 12, for a way to unfold the critic's message.)

CONCLUSION

Mama Slinky

The one idea or feeling or sense that I wish to offer you in this book is the fact that the Intentional Field is a guiding force that is always there, night or day. It is a wellspring from which our creativity arises. Without contact with its everlasting flow, life can feel dull or static. When we're connected to it, life is a pulsing stream of constant discovery and wonder. We do not have to look far for its inspiration. It is always there in the slightest things that catch our attention. Nature is continually generous; we merely have to open our eyes and hearts to its gifts.

I hope this book has given you a glimpse of the infinite expressions of the Intentional Field and has encouraged you to join it, to ride its waves, to dive into its murk and magic and discover new worlds appearing in the form of puppets, music, writing, relationships, or just answering the mail.

Whether the exercises have inspired you to discover a truck driver or a "mama slinky," a flying machine or a stuffy critic, a silly animal or a passionate song—remember that it is not only the concrete creations and figures that are important and fun, but that you can return, again and again, to the very seed from which they came.

BIBLIOGRAPHY

Watchful

Allison, Drew, and Donald Devet. *The Foam Book: An Easy Guide to Building Polyfoam Puppets.* Charlottesville, N.C.: Grey Seal Puppets, 2002.

Arye, Lane. *Unintentional Music: Releasing Your Deepest Creativity.* Charlottesville, Virginia: Hampton Roads, 2001.

Audergon, Arlene. "Process Acting." *The Journal of Process Oriented Psychology* 6 (1994–1995): 63-72.

Barron, Frank, Alfonso Montuori, and Anthea Barron, eds. *Creators on Creating: Awakening and Cultivating the Imaginative Mind.* New York: Jeremy Tarcher/Putnam, 1977.

Blumenthal, Eileen, and Julie Taymor. *Playing with Fire.* rev. ed. New York: Harry Abrams, 1999.

Brook, Peter. "Lie and Glorious Adjective: An Interview with Peter Brook." *Parabola* (Summer 1981): 60-73.

Byrd, Jeffery. "Cage, John." *glbtq.com* ("an encyclopedia of gay, lesbian, bisexual, transgender, & queer culture"), http://www.glbtq.com/arts/cage_j.html

Carter, Chris, and Stephen Carter. *Creatures of Whimsy: The Art of Basil Milovsoroff (1906–1992)*. Seattle: Northwest Puppet Center, and Pixel Productions, 1998. Videocasette.

Chamberlain, Franc. *Michael Chekhov*. London: Routledge, 2004.

Chekhov, Michael. *To the Actor: On the Technique of Acting*. London: Routledge, 2002.

Clark, Laura and Suzanne Brown. *Taoism*. http://mcel.pacificu.edu/as/students/vb/Taoism.htm

Dolen, Christine. "Queen of the Jungle." *Miami Herald Tribune*, 20 October 2002. (http://www.broward.com/mld/miamiherald/entertainment/columnists/christine_dolen/4315872.htm).

Feynman, Richard."The Dignified Professor." In *Creators on Creating: Awakening and Cultivating the Imaginative Mind*, edited by Frank Barron, Alfonso Montuori, and Anthea Barron. New York: Jeremy Tarcher/Putnam, 1977.

Ghiselin, Brewster. *The Creative Process: Reflections on Invention in the Arts and Sciences*. Berkeley, California: University of California Press, 1985.

Gil, Eliana. *Play in Family Therapy*. New York: Guildford Press, 1994.

Goodbread, Joseph. *The Dreambody Toolkit: A Practical Introduction to the Philosophy, Goals and Practice of Process-Oriented Psychology*. 2nd ed. Portland, Oregon: Lao Tse Press, 1997.

Greenberg, Robert. "Lecture 8: Style Features of Baroque Music and a Brief Tutorial on Pitch, Motive, Melody, and Texture." *How to Listen to and Understand Great Music*. The Teaching Company, 1998. Audiocassette.

Halprin, Anna. *Dance as a Healing Art*. Kentfield, California: Tamalpa Institute, 1997.

Henson, Cheryl, and the Muppet Workshop. *The Muppets Make Puppets*. New York: Workman Publishing, 1994.

The Academician

Hoff, Benjamin. *The Tao of Pooh*. New York: Penguin, 1983.

Inches, Alison. *Jim Henson's Designs and Doodles: A Muppet Sketch-book*. New York: Harry N. Abrams, Inc., 2001.

IONE. *Listening in Dreams: A Compendium of Sound Dreams, Meditations and Rituals for Deep Dreamers*. New York: iUniverse, 2005.

Jenkins, Ron. "Two Way Mirrors." *Parabola*, (August, 1981): 17–21.

Joyce, Cynthia. "I like to Make Steps," interview with Merce Cunningham. *Salon.com.* http://www.salon.com/weekly/interview960722.html

Kalff, Dora. *Sandplay: A Psychotherapeutic Approach to the Psyche*. Santa Monica, California: Sigo Press, 1980.

Khan, Hazrat Inayat. *The Mysticism of Sound and Music*. rev. ed. Boston: Shambhala, 1996.

Kinberg, Judy (producer-director), and Sara Lukinson (writer-coproducer). *The World of Jim Henson*. Great Performances/PBS, 1995. Videocassette.

Laybourne, Kit. *The Animation Book: A Complete Guide to Animated Filmmaking: From Flip-Books to Sound Cartoons to 3-D Animation*. New York: Three Rivers Press, 1998.

Mu

Marshall, Lorna and David Williams. "Peter Brook: Transparency and the Invisible Network." In *Twentieth Century Actor Training*, edited by Alison Hodge, 174-190. New York: Routledge, 2000.

McCutchan, Ann. *The Muse That Sings: Composers Speak about the Creative Process.* New York: Oxford University Press, 1999.

McDermott, Phelim, and Julian Crouch. "Puppetry: A User's Guide."   http://www.improbable.co.uk/article.asp?article_id=3

Michalko, Michael. *Cracking Creativity: The Secrets of Creative Genius.* Berkeley, California: Ten Speed Press, 2001.

Mindell, Amy. "A Brief Review of Recent Evolution in Process Theory." *The Journal of Process Oriented Psychology* 9, (Summer 2004).

———. *Alternative to Therapy.* Newport, Oregon: Zero Publications, 2002.

———. "Amy's Hyperspaces: Creativity, the Bird of Paradise, and the Doorway to Parallel Worlds." Article on author's website (http://www.aamindell.net/research_frame.htm), 2002.

————. *Metaskills: The Spiritual Art of Therapy.* Tempe, Arizona: New Falcon Press, 1994. Reprint. Portland, Oregon: Lao Tse Press, 2003.

————. "Music, Mystery, and the Dreaming Process." *Dream Network Journal* 21, (June 2002): 7–11.

———— and Arnold Mindell. *Riding the Horse Backwards: Process Work in Theory and Practice.* New York: Penguin, 1992. Reprint. Portland, Oregon: Lao Tse Press, 2002.

Mindell, Arnold. *City Shadows: Psychological Interventions in Psychiatry.* New York: Routledge, 1988.

————. *Coma: The Dreambody Near Death.* Boulder: Shambhala Publications, 1989, and London: Penguin-Arkana, 1994. Currently available as an e-book at www.laotse.com

————. *The Deep Democracy of Open Forums.* Charlottesville, Virginia: Hampton Roads, 2002.

————. *Dreambody: The Body's Role in Revealing the Self.* Santa Monica, California: Sigo Press, 1982. Reprint. Portland, Oregon: Lao Tse Press, 1998.

————. *The Dreambody in Relationships.* New York: Penguin, 1987. Reprint. Portland, Oregon: Lao Tse Press, 2002.

————. *Dreaming While Awake: Techniques for 24-Hour Lucid Dreaming.* Charlottesville, Virginia: Hampton Roads, 2000.

————. *The Dreammaker's Apprentice: Using Heightened States of Consciousness to Interpret Dreams.* Charlottesville, Virginia: Hampton Roads, 2001.

————. *The Leader as Martial Artist: An Introduction to Deep Democracy Techniques and Strategies for Resolving Conflict and Creating Community.* San Francisco: HarperCollins, 1992. Reprint. Portland, Oregon: Lao Tse Press, 2000.

————. *Quantum Mind: The Edge between Physics and Psychology.* Portland, Oregon: Lao Tse Press, 2000.

Wise Owl

————. *The Quantum Mind and Healing: How to Listen and Respond to Your Body's Symptoms*. Charlottesville, Virginia: Hampton Roads, 2004..

————. *River's Way: The Process Science of the Dreambody*. London: Routledge & Kegan Paul, 1985

————. *The Shaman's Body: A New Shamanism forTransforming Health, Relationships, and Community*. San Francisco: Harper-Collins, 1993/1996.

————. *The Shaman's World: Paths of Creation in Psychology, Spirituality, and Physics*. Forthcoming.

————. *Sitting in the Fire: Large Group Transformation through Diversity and Conflict*. Portland, Oregon: Lao Tse Press, 1995.

————. "Some History, Theory and Practice Beginning with the Dreambody and Including the Quantum Mind and Healing." Article on author's website (http://www.aamindell.net/processwork_frame.htm), 2004.

————. *Working on Yourself Alone: Inner Dreambody Work*. New York: Penguin, 1991. Reprint. Portland, Oregon: Lao Tse Press, 2002.

Baby Star King

———. *Working with the Dreaming Body.* London, England: Penguin-Arkana, 1984. Reprint. Portland, Oregon: Lao Tse Press, 2002.

———. *The Year I: Global Process Work with Planetary Tensions.* New York: Penguin-Arkana, 1989.

Oliveros, Pauline. Website: *Deep Listening: A Composer's Sound Practice.* New York: iUniverse, 2005.

Rosenblum, Robert. *Cubism and Twentieth-Century Art.* New York: Harry N. Abrams, 2001.

Schechner, Richard. "Julie Taymor: From Jacques Lecoq to *The Lion King*," interview with Julie Taymor in *Puppets, Masks and Performing Objects.* ed. John Bell. Cambridge, Massachusetts: MIT Press, 2001.

Schupbach, Max. "Process Work." In *Handbook of Complementary and Alternative Therapies in Mental Health,* edited by S. Shannon, 355-373. San Diego: Academic Press, 2002.

Straub, Sonja. "Stalking Your Inner Critic: A Process-Oriented Approach to Self-Criticism." Unpublished thesis, Research Society for Process Oriented Psychology, 1990.

Stravinsky, Igor. *Poetics of Music: In the Form of Six Lessons.* Cambridge, Massachusetts: Harvard University Press, 1970.

Suzuki, Shunryu. *Zen Mind, Beginner's Mind*. New York: Weatherhill, 1970.

Tharp, Twyla. *The Creative Habit: Learn It and Use It for Life*. New York: Simon & Schuster, 2003.

Thomas, Bob. *Disney's Art of Animation: From Mickey Mouse to Beauty and the Beast*. New York: Hyperion, 1991.

Viereck, G.S. "What Life Means to Einstein: An Interview by George Sylvester Viereck." *The Saturday Evening Post*, October 26, 1929.

Wennstrom, Jerry. *The Inspired Heart: An Artist's Journey of Transformation*. Boulder, Colorado: Sentient Publications, 2002.

Wirth, Jason. *Zen No Sho: The Calligraphy of Fukushima Keido Roshi*. Santa Fe, New Mexico: Clear Light Books, 2003.

Zollo, Paul. *Songwriters on Songwriting*. rev. ed. New York: Da Capo Press, 1997.

INDEX

A

altered states, 153
    parallel worlds, 154
animation, 35
    stop motion, 100
amplifying, 223
awareness, 22
    boundaries of, 97
    lucid, 57
    subtle, 22

B

beginner's mind, 56
Brook, Peter, 121
blocked,
    creativity, 79, 103, 140, 201-203, 223
    mood, 209
    therapist, 210
body,
    artistic canvas, as, 179
    feeling, 114
    imaginary, 154
    inner tendencies, 69
    subtle sensations, 81
    symptoms, 37, 179

C

Cage, John, 139
channels, 154
    switching, 226
Chekhov, Michael, 35
    imaginary body, 154
childhood,
    play, 79
clay, 61
cloudy mind, 56
Consensus Reality, 20
    Intentional Field, 223
    Primary Process, 20

creativity, 2, 6, 59
    blocked, 79, 103140, 201, 223
    environment, 111-113
    figure, 159
    flickers, 71
    Flirts, 111
    hidden, 22
    impasse, 135, 140, 201
    impulse, 72
    inner critic, 103, 201
    Intentional Field, 2, 7, 142
    It, 79
    mask, 124
    mind, 56
    mundane, 66
    parallel worlds, 157
    perception, 153
    play, 99
    project, 114
    puppets, 77, 83, 97, 155
    Stravinsky, Igor, 95
    story, 168
    time, 7
    uncreative, 217
critic,
    mood, 209
    motivation, 211
    voice, 226
cubism, 153

D

dance, 44
    choreography, 157
    expression, 99
    improvisational, 140
    parallel worlds, 154
    puppets, 85
    stop motion animation, 100
democracy,
    fluid, 91

inner critic, 103
many dimensions, 91
dimensions of experience, 20
    changing, 154
    channels, 91
    Consensus Reality, 152
    Dreamland, 152
    Essence, 152
    flowing through, 59
    switching, 91
dream, 81
    childhood, 23
    figure, 153
    mask, 125
    world, 180
Dreambody, 3
    puppets, 179
Dreaming, 8
    Aboriginal, 22
    everyday, 122
    matter, in, 3
    moment, in, 72
    puppets, 85
    weaves dreams, 139
Dreaming process, 4, 5
    identity, and, 127
    secret, 86
    symptoms, 180
Dreamland, 19-23, 37, 60
    Essence, 154
    Intentional Field, 223
    moods, 211

E
edge,
    process, of, 226
    unfold, 223
empty mind, 57, 114, 121, 141-142
environment, 112-113
    creativity, 112-113
    flirting with, 111, 113
    inspiration, 111
    sounds, 169-170
Essence, 20-23, 31, 36, 59

art, 31
    critic, 37, 205
    music, 165
    resolution, 180-182
    symptom, in, 180, 187
experience,
    see dimensions of

F
fairy tale,
    Intentional Field, 139, 142
figures,
    dream, 153
    mood, 210
    parallel world, 159
    puppets, 82-84
Flirts, 20, 23, 44, 55-66
    attention, 142
    environment, 111, 113
    lucid attention, 176
    mask, 121
    materials, 111, 124
    next step, 107
    rhythm, 165
    sounds, 170
    unfold, 96
    visual, 144
    words, 143
flow, 25-26
    creative, 79
    Intentional Field, 81
    invisible, 15
    life, 18
    through dimensions, 59
fluidity, 23
    deeply democratic, 91
Flying Umbrella,
    dream, 140
    exercise, 140
    group, 143
    story, 139
foam, 59-60
foggy mind, 56-57, 61, 96, 114, 121,
    142, 144

Fukushima Roshi, 33, 36, 56

G

group process,
    Flying Umbrella, 143
    puppets, 85

H

haiku, 33

I

I Ching, 25
    music, 140
identity,
    primary, 170
ideograph, 32-33
    musical, 165
impasse,
    creative, 135, 140, 201
Improbable Theatre, 95
initiation,
    masks, 121
inspiration, 229
    environment, 111
Intentional Field, 5, 15, 18-24, 31,
    38, 59, 63, 65
    awareness, 180
    Consensus Reality, in, 223
    creativity, 2, 7, 142
    critic part, 103
    Dreamland, in, 223
    fairy tale, 139, 142
    flow, 80
    force, 81
    parameters, 140
    puppets, 95
    relationships, 181
    story, 142
It, 79, 103, 140, 176, 181, 201-202

L

later,
    I'll do it, 71-73
life, 18, 85
    creative, 213

Essence, 187
    everyday, 59, 95, 187, 213
    generative, 217
    Intentional Field, 213
    meaning for, 100, 128
    puppets, 101
life force,
    "inanimate" objects, 91
    inherent, 91
    within materials, 22
lucidity, 56-57
    attention, 57, 107, 176
    Dreaming, 5
    Flirts, 176

M

magic, 55, 57-59, 121
    Dreamworld, 180
marginalized,
    creative energy, 71
    Essence, 179
    Intentional Field, 187
    parallel worlds, 152
mask,
    animals, 121
    behind, 119
    ceremonies, 121
    cross-cultural, 121
    dream, 122-127
    everyday, 125
    Flirts, 121
    hand, 119
    initiation, 121
    ordinary identity, 121, 125-
    127
    paper bag, 96
    paper plate, 122
    rituals, 121
    spirits, 121
meditation, 140
    mask, 124, 127, 131
mess,
    making, 217
metaphor,

life, 143
metaskill, 25, 57
    compassion, 57
    devotion, 59
    love, 57
    mother, 80
    openness, 152
    playful, 140
    preciousness, 80
    tenderness, 80
    unreal as real, 96
    wonder, 80
mood,
    exercise, 210
    inner critic, 103, 209
    music, 209
    puppets, 211
motifs, 166
    movement, 166
    musical, 33-35, 166, 169
movement, 63
    critic, 204
    Intentional Field, 16
    micro, 84, 204
    rhythm, 114
    subtle, 129
    tendencies, 129
music, 25, 151
    Essence, 165
    expression, 99
    mask, 131
    moods, 209
    motifs, 33-35, 166, 169
    parallel worlds, 154, 165
    parameters, 140
    song, 114, 124

N
nonconsensual, 20

P
painting,
    Asian, 33
parallel worlds, 23, 63, 153

creativity, 154, 157
    figure, 159
    identity, 125
    musical, 165
    personal processes, 166
    puppets, 81
parameters, 23-25, 35
    Intentional Field, 140
    sock, 79
pattern,
    automatic, 125
    life, 23, 64
personalities,
    puppets, 81
play, 23-25, 140
    children, 79
    creativity, 99
    therapist, 86
poem, 99, 114
    rhythm, 114
    mask, 124
process,
    oriented psychology, 3
    primary, 20, 125, 153, 166
    secondary, 153, 166
puppeteer, 85, 180
puppets, 31, 77, 81
    advisor, as, 84
    create, 97
    critic, 86
    dance, 84-85
    Dreambody, 179-181
    Dreaming, 85
    group process, 85
    Intentional Field, 95
    moods, 209, 211
    paper plate, 180
    personalities, 81
    roles, 86
    shadow, 180
    singing, 84
    socks, 77-81
    stop-motion animation, 100
    supervisors, as, 86

therapy, 86
writing, 84

R

rhythm, 114
    attention, 166
    critic, 204
    Flirt, 165
    poem, 114
relationship, 22, 125
    mask to mask, 127
    puppet, 85
roles,
    playing, 154
    puppets play, 86
    switch, 127

S

sandbox, 25
seed,
    creative projects, 111
    critic, 201-203
    Essence, 202
    experience, 22, 189
    Intentional Field, 201
    movement, 170
    sound, 170
sentient, 20
    feeling, 80, 127
shadow puppets,
    Indonesia, 180
shapeshift, 122
shy,
    being puppet, 83
    puppets, 86, 211
signals,
    double, 154
    moment-to-moment, 223
    sensory grounded, 223
    unintended, 153
song,
    critic, 6
    rhythm, 114
    unfold, 114

sound, 166
    Flirts, 170
    mood, 210
    movement, 166
    parallel, 168
    secondary, 169
    unintentional, 169
stop-motion animation,
    puppets, 100-102
story,
    complete, 144
    create, 168
    expression, 99
    Intentional Field, 139
    unfold, 131
subtle tendencies, 20
symbolic,
    answer, 144
    solution, 143

T

theater,
    improvisational, 140
    masks, 121
    parallel worlds, 154

U

uncarved block, 61
unfolding, 61
    amplifying, 223
    awareness, 224
    creative idea, 72
    edge, 224
    Essence, 204
    Flirts, 96
    process, 226
    relationship, 80
    song, 124
    story, 131, 144

W

writing,
    Intentional Field, 99
    puppets, 84